ADVANCE PRAISE FOR *DEBT FREE FOR LIFE*

"David Bach has changed the lives and taught millions to be smarter with their money and live a truly rich life through his 10 national bestselling books and regular appearances on NBC's *Today* show and the *Oprah* show. He has now taken his honest, simple, 'take action' advice to inspire and teach America to shed its debt with his latest book, *Debt Free for Life*. David has created the ultimate debt guide with the latest and greatest systems and tools to achieve financial freedom once and for all. *Debt Free for Life* is about gaining back ownership of your life and creating a brighter, financially secure future."

—Susan C. Keating, President and CEO of the
National Foundation for Credit Counseling

"David Bach understands the struggle of millions of people who are drowning in debt and has written the must-read of the decade to inspire and guide us to shed our debt—FOR GOOD! *Debt Free for Life* provides actionable advice and SOLUTIONS—what you can do TODAY to fix your finances and fix your debt. Bach's plan includes an abundance of tools to lead to a debt-free world of true financial security. Pick up your copy of *Debt Free for Life* today and join David's mission to turn back the tide of debt and buy back our futures—futures free from debt."

—David C. Jones, President of the Association of
Independent Consumer Credit Counseling Agencies

PRAISE FOR *THE AUTOMATIC MILLIONAIRE*

"*The Automatic Millionaire* is an automatic winner. David Bach really cares about you: on every page you can hear him cheering you on to financial fitness. No matter who you are or what your income is, you can benefit from this easy-to-apply program. Do it now. You and your loved ones deserve big bucks!"   —Ken Blanchard, coauthor of *The One Minute Manager®*

"*The Automatic Millionaire* gives you, step by step, everything you need to secure your financial future. When you do it David Bach's way, failure is not an option."   —Jean Chatzky, Financial Editor, NBC's *Today*

"David Bach's no spin financial advice is beautiful because it's so simple. If becoming self-sufficient is important to you, then this book is a must."
—Bill O'Reilly, anchor, Fox News, and author of
The O'Reilly Factor and *The No Spin Zone*

PRAISE FOR *START LATE, FINISH RICH*

"Financial wizard David Bach's new book, *Start Late, Finish Rich*, offers solid advice for getting our finances in order, no matter how old we are."
—AARP

"With feel-good sensibilities, David Bach delivers levelheaded strategies for reaching financial goals. . . . Bach's clever approach will make readers feel as if they're having a one-on-one conversation with a friendly personal financial counselor. . . . Powerful, poignant and pleasing, *Start Late, Finish Rich* can't be read fast enough."   —*Bookpage*

PRAISE FOR *SMART COUPLES FINISH RICH*

"*Smart Couples Finish Rich* teaches women and men to work together as a team when it comes to money. Bach's nine steps are powerful, yet easy to understand and fun to implement. The entire family can benefit from this great book."   —Robert T. Kiyosaki, author of *Rich Dad, Poor Dad*

"I know how hard it is to make a personal-finance book user-friendly. Bach has done it. *Smart Couples Finish Rich* picks up where *Smart Women Finish Rich* left off. . . . This is an easy, lively read filled with tips that made me smile and at least once made me laugh."   —*USA Weekend*

"David Bach offers a prescription both to avoid money conflicts and to plan a harmonious future together. . . . The bottom line is action, and Bach's chatty writing style helps motivate you to that end."   —*BusinessWeek*

PRAISE FOR *SMART WOMEN FINISH RICH*

"Inspires women to start planning today for a secure financial future. Every woman can benefit from this book. . . . Bach is an excellent money coach."
—John Gray, bestselling author of
Men Are from Mars, Women Are from Venus

"David Bach is the one expert to listen to when you're intimidated by your finances. His easy-to-understand program will show you how to afford your dreams."
—Anthony Robbins, author of *Awaken the Giant Within*
and *Unlimited Power*

"[David] Bach gets across some complicated stuff: how to organize a portfolio, keep the taxman at bay, invest in yourself, and earn more, all of which makes this book one of the best overall." —*Working Woman*

PRAISE FOR *THE AUTOMATIC MILLIONAIRE HOMEOWNER*

"[Bach's] cheery, can-do message . . . cuts through the intimidating challenge of buying a house for the first-timer . . . for a newcomer, it's fundamental reading." —*USA Today*

"If you read only one real estate book this year, it should be *The Automatic Millionaire Homeowner* . . . This is one of the few real estate books that cannot be recommended too highly for both beginners and experienced homeowners." —Robert J. Bruss, *Miami Herald*

PRAISE FOR *GO GREEN, LIVE RICH*

"Great news: there is no green premium! By demonstrating how going green can fit any budget, David Bach shows that good environmental and financial decisions go hand-in-hand. *Go Green, Live Rich* gives great tips, useful to everyone, about how to save money and the planet at once."
—Robert F. Kennedy Jr.

"*Go Green, Live Rich* is as much about saving money as it is about preserving our world of natural wonders for future generations. This is the rich-green book of a promising tomorrow."
—Matthew Modine, Founder: Bicycle for a Day

DEBT FREE
FOR LIFE

DEBT FREE FOR LIFE

The Finish Rich Plan for Financial Independence

DAVID BACH

DOUBLEDAY CANADA

Doubleday Canada and colophon are registered trademarks.

Library and Archives of Canada Cataloguing in Publication has been applied for

ISBN: 978-0-385-66625-1

The Automatic Millionaire Homeowner, The Automatic Millionaire, The Latte Factor, Smart Women Finish Rich, Smart Couples Finish Rich, and DOLP are registered trademarks of FinishRich Media, LLC.

This book is designed to provide accurate and authoritative information on the subject of personal finances. While all of the stories and anecdotes described in the book are based on true experiences, most of the names are pseudonyms, and some situations have been changed slightly for educational purposes and to protect each individual's privacy. It is sold with the understanding that neither the Author nor the Publisher is engaged in rendering legal, accounting, or other professional services by publishing this book. As each individual situation is unique, questions relevant to personal finances and specific to the individual should be addressed to an appropriate professional to ensure that the situation has been evaluated carefully and appropriately. The Author and Publisher specifically disclaim any liability, loss, or risk which is incurred as a consequence, directly or indirectly, of the use and application of any of the contents of this work.

Printed and bound in the USA

Published in Canada by Doubleday Canada,
a division of Random House of Canada Limited

Visit Random House of Canada Limited's website: www.randomhouse.ca

10 9 8 7 6 5 4 3 2 1

To Alatia, Jack, and James, thank you for making my life so meaningful, and joyful—you are my life's greatest blessings.

I love you with all my heart.

CONTENTS

ACKNOWLEDGEMENTS

Truly to my readers, THANK YOU, THANK YOU, THANK YOU! It is hard sometimes for me to believe that *Debt Free For Life* is my twelfth book in the FinishRich Series—and that there are now more than seven million of the FinishRich books in print around the world. So, I want to start by first thanking YOU, my readers. As a writer you spend literally thousands of hours often on a book by yourself—and then you wait and wonder if what you wrote really makes a difference? Fortunately for me, so many of you write to me on a daily basis that I know my work is helping you, and for that I am deeply grateful. YOU inspire me to keep doing what I do. I am deeply humbled and grateful for your trust, your love, and your constant encouragement. THANK YOU sounds small, but it is truly coming from my heart, and if I could give each and every one of you a hug or high five, I would! Thousands of you have asked me to write this book, and I truly hope it meets your expectations and helps you. I take your investment of your money and, most important, your time and trust seriously, and I am again so grateful that you continue to follow me from book to book.

I am equally grateful to the many people who have worked so tirelessly with me over the years to support my message of financial hope and action. I feel incredibly fortunate to have so many dedicated colleagues who truly care about making a difference in the world. There are so many of you to thank, and what follows is only a short list, but please know if I have left you out of this acknowledgment, you are still in my heart and prayers.

I want first to start by thanking Oprah Winfrey. The opportunity to reach your millions of viewers allowed me to help millions more people than I could have ever dreamed possible. I am literally thanked weekly by readers who say, "I saw you on *Oprah,* and changed my life because of what you said on her show." I will always be grateful to you and your world-class team at Harpo for giving me the platform to teach people all over the world how to be smarter with their money. The Debt Diet Series I did with you inspired me to spend the last five years teaching America how to get out of debt and led directly to this book. To Katy Davis, Candy Carter and Dana Brooks, and your fabulous teams who helped us make all of our shows together so powerful, you are my guiding angels. Thank you for believing in me and my message.

To the team at NBC's *Today* show, I am so grateful to all of you for giving me the incredible opportunity to be a weekly contributor to your "Money 911" segments for the past two years. Getting to answer America's financial questions each week has been an amazing experience. A special thank-you to Marc Victor, Jacklyn Levin, Gil Reisfield, Amanda Avery, Katherine Buckley, Elizabeth Neumann, Donna Nicholls, and Michele Leone for your production expertise and the hard work you do to make these segments as fantastic as they are. A big thank-you to Matt Lauer, Meredith Vieira, Ann Curry, and Natalie Morales for being so wonderful to work with. And a special hug to Al Roker—you make each week a blast! And to Jean Chatzky, Sharon Epperson, and Carmen Ulrich Wong—you are world-class experts who make each show fantastic.

To Allan Mayer, we've worked together now for well over a decade. Words can't express how grateful I am for our incredible working relationship. Your feedback is invaluable and you make me better each time you edit my books. Thank you so much for making this, our ninth book together, go so smoothly. To Zac Bissonette and Helen Huntley, thank you for your contributions to this book.

To Stephen Breimer, thank you once again for your unceasing efforts to protect and promote my brand and business. Every day I thank my lucky stars that you represent me. Kudos to you, my friend—I salute you!

To my new partners at Equifax and the DebtWise.com team, I can't wait to spread our message about the "Debt Free Challenge." We have set a huge goal for ourselves to inspire a million people to get out of debt in 2011—and I am looking forward to the journey! To BKV and Jackson Spalding, your work is truly outstanding. Here's to a very successful and fun launch.

To my team at Random House, this is our eleventh book together! I am incredibly grateful that I have been in business with the same publisher my entire career. I deeply appreciate your commitment to me as an author. You have worked tirelessly to make my books the best of their kind in the industry. A special thanks to my new publisher Tina Constable, editor Roger Scholl, marketing director Meredith McGinnis, and publicist Tara Gilbride. To Chris Fortunato, for his tireless efforts to crash-complete the book packaging, you always rise to the occasion—thank you. To David Drake, head of publicity—you rock, sir! You are the best in the business, and I am grateful to have been working with you since 1997. Thank you, thank you—really, thank you!

To my right hands at FinishRich Media, Molly and Brittney—ladies, you are simply the best. Thank you for everything you do to keep me on schedule, pumped up, and running fast. You make doing what I do a joy!

To my parents, Bobbi and Marty, I love you both so much. Thank you for always believing in me and encouraging me. I am blessed to have parents who love me so much. To my grandma, Rose Goldsmith, you are the most dear grandmother anyone could ever ask for. To my little sister, Emily Bach, a special big hug to you. I love you so much.

To my sons, Jack and James, my little boys who soon will not be so little—your daddy loves you more than the sun, the moon, and the stars. You boys are my greatest joy. To Alatia Bradley, my sweetheart, soul mate, and best friend—thank you for making every day and everything better. I truly feel each and every day grateful that you came into my life. I love you!

To my EO buddies, David Rich, Roark Dunn, Brian Martin, Jay Kubasssek, Chris Power, Andrew Christodoulides, Navid Moradi, Mitch Schamroth, Laurence Levi, you guys have been my business soul mates. Thank you for your friendship and constant encouragement!

And again, lastly to you, my readers. I could fill this page with "thank you"s and it wouldn't begin to express how deeply grateful and blessed I feel to be able to do what I do for you. You made it all possible. I am humbled by your faith and trust in me—and thankful for how many of you regularly take the time to email me your success stories. I can't reply to every email I get, but I do read them all, and I am truly grateful on a daily basis for your words of encouragement and your good wishes! I thank you from the bottom of my heart.

David Bach
New York
September 2010

INTRODUCTION

GOODBYE, DEBT—HELLO, FREEDOM!

Early in the winter of 2010, I was sitting in the greenroom preparing to go on the NBC's *Today* show to do our weekly "Money 911" segment. The segment had been airing for more than two years. Each week we would take questions from viewers about their money. This week, most of the questions seemed to be about debt. Reading over the questions, it hit me—in just two years, we had gone from being asked mainly about investments to being asked almost entirely about personal debt.

As I thought about this, a friend in the greenroom interrupted me with a question of her own. "David," she asked, "what's your take on *'good debt'* vs. *'bad debt'*?"

Almost automatically, I started giving her the standard answer about how good debts are generally considered to be debts you incur to buy things that can go up in value—like a home or a college education—while bad debts are things such as credit card balances, where you've borrowed money to buy things that will go down in value, like most consumer goods. But then I stopped mid-answer and looked at her.

"You know something?" I said. "The truth is that this recession has changed everything. Homes are going down in value and people with college degrees are looking for jobs. Forget what I was just telling you. Forget about the idea of 'good debt' and 'bad debt.' The truth is that when you're in debt, it doesn't matter what you've borrowed the money for. The only thing that matters is whether or not you can afford to pay it back. And if you can't, *all* debt is bad debt."

My friend smiled sadly. "Tell me about it," she said. "My home is underwater, and my mortgage rate is going up and I can't refinance because my credit score has dropped." She shook her head and sighed.

"So what do I do? *What's your advice to people like me?*"

THE BEST INVESTMENT YOU CAN MAKE NOW

This time I stopped and thought before answering. "Here's what I think," I finally said, "and this is what I'm going to be telling everyone now. **The best investment you can make over the next ten years is going to be paying off your debts. So my advice is to pay off what you owe as fast as you can.** The faster you pay off your debt, the faster you will achieve financial freedom."

I went on to tell my friend that at Morgan Stanley, where I had worked as a financial advisor for nearly a decade, the clients of ours who focused on paying off their debt were able to retire an average of ten years earlier than those who didn't.

"So does this mean I should stop putting money into my retirement plan and instead use it to pay off my mortgage?" she asked.

I shook my head. "Of course not," I replied. "You should never stop 'paying yourself first.' What you need to do is cut down your spending so you can stop going into debt, and pay off your debt faster. Trust me—getting out of debt has never been more important than it is now. Being *debt free for life* should be your new financial goal."

And with that I headed into the studio with Al Roker to answer the nation's never-ending questions about debt.

ARE YOU TIRED OF BEING IN DEBT?
DO YOU WANT A NEW WAY OUT?

If you're like most people, you're probably familiar with the idea of "good debt" and "bad debt." Millions of Canadians believe in this idea. In fact, millions of Canadians have based their lives on it. At the heart of this belief is the notion that good debt makes you rich and bad debt keeps you poor. You borrow only to buy assets, and you shouldn't borrow to buy things that drop in value. It makes sense; it seems logical.

I, too, used to believe it. But you know what? I no longer do. And neither should you. Why? *Because the idea that there's such a thing as good debt and bad debt is a myth.*

The truth is, we've been misled.

- We've been misled by millions of dollars worth of advertising that gets us to buy things we don't really need.

- We've been misled by a multi-billion-dollar credit card industry that tells us the good life can be ours for the taking when we use their credit cards.

- We've been misled by lenders who promoted the idea that we were "silly" to keep equity in our homes when we could "cash it out" to pay off our credit cards.

- We were sold a bill of goods—or, more accurately, a bill of loans (billions of dollars of them). And now this bill has come due, and our debt has become our personal financial prison.

Are you tired of being in debt? Are you tired of waking up each morning to face an ever-larger pile of bills? Like my friend in the greenroom, do you find yourself working harder than ever to pay for things you no longer care about—or even want to own?

If so, you are not alone. Millions of people feel the same way—and like you, they are ready for a life free from debt. *A life where you own your life—rather than lease it.*

The good news is that there is a way out of this nightmare. There is a better way to live—starting today—a way that will allow you to be debt free for life!

THE MIRACLE OF COMPOUND INTEREST— IN REVERSE!

Here's the truth: DEBT IS DEBT. Probably the most important lesson of the great recession we've just lived through is that there's no such thing as a good debt if you can't afford to pay it off. When you can't make the payments, the only difference between "good" debts and "bad" debts is that the bad variety can destroy your financial life much more quickly.

Now don't get me wrong. We need to be able to borrow money. Without a lending industry and the ability to borrow, we could not function as a society. Borrowing to build assets can make sense—*if you have a real plan to repay your debt.* But if you don't have a plan, look out! Debt is all about basic math. It is the miracle of compound interest in reverse, which is to say that if you don't stay on top of it, it will mushroom faster than you can imagine—and crush you before you know what's happening.

This is one big reason I wrote this book: to give you the plan you need to pay off your debts faster than you would ever have thought possible.

DEBT FREE FOR LIFE:
A NEW APPROACH AND A NEW ATTITUDE

It is time for us to rethink entirely the way we manage our money and our debt. If the great recession has taught us anything, it is that the less debt we have, the better off we are. With this in mind, I am now on a mission to inspire you to shed your debt. I believe it is time for us to buy back our freedom, and I know that together we can do it. This is another reason I have written *Debt Free for Life*—and why I hope you will read it and act on its advice starting today.

Debt Free for Life is my twelfth book in twelve years. It is very possible that you have read (or at least heard of) one of my previous titles. As I write this, there are more than 7 million copies of my FinishRich books in print around the world. I am known for my honest, simple, and "take action" advice about finances, and I've been privileged to inspire millions around the world to be smarter with their money and truly live a rich life. Perhaps you have seen me on television on NBC's *Today* show, "Money 911" segments, or on Oprah's "Debt Diet" series, or on CNBC's "The Millionaire Inside." Then again, maybe this is our first visit together—and, if it is, welcome! In either case, I want to say, THANK YOU. Thank you for your time and your trust that I may have a plan for you—a plan that will make you DEBT FREE FOR LIFE!

ELIMINATE YOUR DEBT—
AND BUY BACK YOUR FREEDOM!

So why did I pick this moment to write a book on getting out of debt—and why should you spend a few hours reading it? Why is it time to buy back our freedom and focus on our own personal economy?

The answer is simple:

In our new economy, getting out of debt fast is the most important financial move you and your family can make.

There are three reasons for this.

First, I believe that our debt is out of control.

Every day I get tons of questions from my readers—maybe you're one of them—and most of them are related to debt. You email me at **www.finishrich.com**, you post at my community at **www.facebook.com/davidbach**, and you call in to the various shows I do. What I hear from you is scary. You've got credit card balances you can't pay off, mortgage loans and home equity lines that are crushing you, student loans, car loans, medical debt—you name it. "David," I hear over and over again, "I'm drowning—what in the world can I do?" Or: "David, I have had enough—**I want to retire someday and not be worried about money—how can I get out of debt once and for all?**" The fact is that we've lost control of our debt both individually and as a nation—and this has to change. We have come to a point in history where personally, nationally, and even globally the devastating effect of debt is beginning not only to crush the human spirit, but also our ability to be free and ultimately secure.

**Second, I believe the world *is* waking up
to the problem of debt.**

National economies around the globe have been shaken to
their core because of debt loads. Europe fears more economic
collapses. Some experts worry that the United States is on the
brink of bankruptcy. Canada has weathered the economic
crisis better than most, but individual Canadians continue to
spend more than they earn in disposable income, and they do
it by going into debt. The ratio of debt to financial assets is
higher among Canadians than in any other of the 20 devloped
countries in the Organisation for Economic Co-operation
and Development (OECD).

Debt has a negative effect on everyone. The debt we have the
best chance of controlling is our own. There are dozens of books
today about "whose fault it is." But I'm not interested in playing
the blame game. We can debate who's to blame for the global
economy's trillion-dollar deficits—or we can focus on our own
families' "deficits" and get our personal finances together. This
book is about SOLUTIONS—what you can do to fix your situation! It's about *you—your* finances—*your* debt! The faster you
are debt free, the faster you will be protected from things you
can't control, like our national budget deficits.

**Third, I am convinced that
MILLIONS ARE READY TO TAKE ACTION.**

Canada has always been more conservative than the United
States when it comes to spending and debt. But even here,
people seem more anxious than ever to pay down debt and
save money. As I write this in the summer of 2010, savings
rates are up to almost 6%, the highest in two decades, and

millions of people, including you, are ready to be debt free. We've had enough of the burden and worry that debt creates. You are ready to take action—smart action—that will help you become financially free and secure. Many of you have written to me, sharing that you are tired of working so hard for so long—and winding up with so little. You are ready to get off the treadmill of going to work, making money, spending money, going to work, making money, spending money. You are ready to be FREE! You are ready for new ideas and new tools that will help you become smarter about your money and your debt. You are ready to be DEBT FREE FOR LIFE!

My previous books contained great tools for debt reduction. But in this new, challenging economy, I realized I needed to create a new, updated plan with the latest and greatest systems to help you get out of debt TODAY. So welcome! Let's spend a few hours together—and get going on a new plan that will lead you to a debt-free world of true financial security. It may not be as easy to get out of debt as it was to get in, but trust me—the benefits that will come from this journey you're about to begin will be more than worth the effort.

Do you believe as I do? Do these three beliefs of mine make sense to you at a gut level? If they do, then please keep reading. Together, we can turn back this tide of debt and buy back our futures. **It is time for a better way of life—one free from debt.**

MY GIFT TO YOU

**THE DEBT FREE FOR LIFE CHALLENGE VIDEO SERIES
AT WWW.FINISHRICH.COM**

I always love to give my readers a free gift. So if you are already feeling inspired to live a debt-free life, I want to encourage you (right now!) to go online to my website at **www.finishrich.com** and join our FinishRich Community. Register and I will send you my *Debt Free for Life Challenge* video series for free—and also give you access to an amazing array of tools we've designed to help you stay motivated to get out of debt.

Through our website you can access "The David Bach Debt Free Challenge" site, an online community where you can interact with like-minded people committed to becoming debt free. Our goal is to inspire one million people to join us on this challenge. On the website, you'll find videos, audios, and interviews with me and other experts to help you live debt free for life. You'll also find contests you can enter to win prizes.

SHARE YOUR SUCCESS STORIES—
AND YOUR QUESTIONS

As always, I want to hear from you about how this book affected your life. This book includes real success stories from real people who have achieved the results you may be looking for. Most of these stories came directly from people who wrote to me after reading one of my books and applying what they had learned. You can find hundreds more at **www.finishrich.com**. Read them and ask yourself, "If they can do it, why not me?"

The answer is you can—and I can't wait to hear about it when you do.

So if you have a success story to share, I'd love to know about it—and if you have questions, I want to hear those, too. You can e-mail me directly at **success@finishrich.com.**

Now, are you ready to become debt free for life? Are you ready to buy back your freedom? Great—let's get started on your journey to become DEBT FREE FOR LIFE! Your new plan awaits you in the next chapter.

Live Rich,
David Bach

DEBT FREE FOR LIFE SUCCESS STORY

My wife and I read *The Automatic Millionaire* and *Start Late, Finish Rich* on vacation at the beach in 2008. These books inspired us to greatly accelerate paying off our credit cards and other debt. We used your DOLP system and within 20 months, we had paid off our credit cards and three car loans—almost $65,000 in all— while increasing my wife's retirement plan and continuing to max out mine. With our new-found cash flow from not paying debt, we have also been able to double our charitable giving and we are saving to buy our own beach house, both as an investment and to enjoy for personal use. And the story gets BETTER! Our son Jeremy, who's in the military and deployed in Afghanistan, told me he read *The Automatic Millionaire* and it inspired him to quit smoking, allowing him to save $2,000 annually! From 5,000 miles away—when I was sharing with him the success we're having thanks to *The Automatic Millionaire*—he shouted, "Dad, that's the book I was telling you about!" Thank you again for motivating us and turbo-charging our way out of debt!

**Joseph G.
Detroit, MI**

CHAPTER ONE

WHO PUT CANADA INTO DEBT—AND HOW YOU CAN GET YOURSELF OUT

Once upon a time (in the decades after the Great Depression), Canadians desired a life of financial freedom. To our grand-parents and great-grandparents, this meant staying out of debt. Living through the Great Depression, our great-grand-parents learned the hard way that debt was bad, that owing money could destroy your life. So they paid for things in cash, they bought homes with big down payments, and they worked hard to pay their mortgages off as quickly as possible. They even had "mortgage-burning parties" in their backyards, where they celebrated their FREEDOM from the banks after the last payment was made. As a result, many of them were able to retire in their early sixties without financial worry. Retirement wasn't a dream for our great-grandparents (and often our grandparents, who learned prudent financial behaviour from their parents), it was a promise! For them, the dream was real—you went to work, you worked hard, you saved money, you paid down your debt, and then you retired with a pension and you lived happily ever after.

CANADIANS CARRY $1.4 TRILLION IN DEBT— WE DESERVE BETTER

These days, the dream of financial freedom—freedom from worry, freedom from living paycheque to paycheque—has become a nightmare. We bought the myth—or, I should say, we bought the lie and turned it into a myth. As I write this, Statistics Canada reports that Canadians are on the hook for more than *$1.4 TRILLION* in consumer and mortgage debt. This translates to an average of $96,000 of debt per Canadian household. At the beginning of 2010, credit card debt in Canada amounted to $78 billion—about $2,225 for every man, woman, and child in the country. The number of people in Canada who hadn't made a payment on their credit cards in three months or more rose by 50% between 2008 and 2009. At more than 2%, the delinquency rate in Toronto was higher than the Canadian average of 1.7%.

Compared to the United States, Canada remains relatively unscathed by the global recession. Housing prices remain fairly stable, even if housing has become increasingly expensive in places like Toronto and Vancouver. Unemployment rates have fallen, and although many Canadians continue to live paycheque to paycheque, the number of personal bankruptcies in Canada has fallen, as well.

Canada's government incurred a $55-billion deficit in fiscal 2009 to shore up the nation's economy against the aftermath of a worldwide recession, but the government anticipates that it will balance this deficit within five years.

This doesn't mean that Canadians have clear sailing ahead. Housing prices have risen to five times the average after-tax income of Canadian households, and interest rates will likely rise by 2011. For every dollar of income, the average Canadian household carries $1.45 in debt. More than half of employed Canadians say they live paycheque to paycheque. If mortgage rates hit 5.25%, about 375,000 mortgage holders in Canada would have trouble making their payments. So perhaps we should all take a page from the government's book and figure out how to get rid of our debt.

HOW IS YOUR DEBT DOING?

So let's be honest. Do you have more debt than you want?

Chances are, you do—or you wouldn't have picked up this book.

Are you paying a huge percentage of your paycheque each month to just cover the interest on what you've borrowed for your home, your car, your student loans, your credit cards, etc.? Are you frustrated that no matter how hard you try to pay off your debt, it seems to take forever and you don't see any progress happening fast enough? Are you worried about your ability to retire someday because of your debt?

Or is it even worse than that? Are you unable to make even the minimum payments on your loans and find yourself falling behind, with your debt growing? Did you know that if you are carrying $10,000 in credit card debt and your card is charging you 25% interest, and you're making minimum payments, it will take you *more than 50 years* to pay off your debt—without borrowing another penny? Did you know if you have a $250,000 mortgage with a low fixed rate of 6%, paying it off over 30 years will cost you just under $540,000?

HUNDREDS OF THOUSANDS OF CANADIANS ARE IN DEBT AND WANT OUT

The reason I am sharing these figures with you not to be negative or to depress you. What I want to do is start this book and your journey to being debt free for life with the truth. **And the truth is that HUNDREDS OF THOUSANDS of Canadians are hugely in debt and want out!**

A study by the Certified General Accountants of Canada says 20% of Canadians with debt think they have too much and have trouble managing it. These individuals want to improve their financial well-being through debt reduction. Indeed, in the recent rush to take advantage of low mortgage rates by refinancing, many loan applicants have been putting money into their homes—meaning they are reducing the amount they owe—rather than taking money out.

So you see—you're not alone! And like so many others, you can do something quickly to change your situation, reduce your debt, and become DEBT FREE FOR LIFE!

THE DEBT FREE FOR LIFE PROMISE: WHY YOU SHOULD READ THIS BOOK— AND ACT ON IT!

It's easy to get into debt. Getting out is another story. Some so-called debt-settlement companies will market to you and tell you "We can cut your debt in half in minutes and save you thousands of dollars." Sorry, but that's just nonsense!

This book is about the truth. It offers an honest plan that will work—*if you work it!* I know some of you are reading this book because you are really drowning in debt and are looking for a life preserver. If this is your situation, I believe this book can be the life raft that gets you back to dry land. But let me be clear: You don't need to be in over your head to benefit from this book or the Debt Free for Life Plan I'm about to share. This book is about a totally new approach to building financial freedom that stresses "paying down your debt" so you can buy back your freedom. I've been teaching my readers for years how to pay down their debt, and maybe I have taught you already—but the **Debt Free for Life Plan** is a revolutionary new system that that will make paying off your debt easier than it has ever been.

Most people who apply the Debt Free for Life Program I will share in the pages that follow will be able to get themselves out of debt an average of 15 years faster and save themselves at least $30,000 in the process. Some of you will do this even faster than that and be out of debt in as little as seven, five, or even just three years. (I've even seen people get out of debt using these tools in less than a year.) How quickly you can do it will depend on you—on how much debt you have, how much you can cut your expenses, and how fast you want to make it happen.

Some of you have debt that is so long overdue that you can no longer be forced to pay it, and you don't even know it. (You will once you read this book.) Some of you can save six figures by simply applying one idea in this book (you'll find it on page 102 in Chapter Nine).

The fact is that the math of debt is not complicated. You simply need to apply the principals I will share and then, like the Nike slogan says, "Just Do It."

Now don't get me wrong—I am not promising you overnight freedom from debt. But what I can promise is that the moment you start on this plan, you will begin to feel better. Just knowing that you have a plan in place to pay down your debt in the right order, the right way—a plan you can carry out yourself that will save you thousands of dollars in interest fees and cut years off your indebtedness—will truly lighten your burden, however light or heavy it may be.

I also promise you that having less debt will feel GREAT. *Debt creates fear. Not having it creates peace of mind.* This may sound like a cliché, but it's true. When you have less debt, you will feel more FREE. You will have fewer worries, less stress, less tension, fewer fights at home. In short, your life will have less fear and more serenity. Not only that, but you will also be able to build wealth faster.

A DEBT FREE FOR LIFE SUCCESS STORY

I cannot express my gratitude for what your books *Start Late, Finish Rich* and *Smart Women Finish Rich* have done for me. They've helped me change not only my financial life, but my physical life as well. My "latte factor" (the way I wasted money) was food! I could not believe how much I was wasting on "occasional" snacks. It was atrocious—and so was my waist line! The one major thing you said that stuck in my head and changed my actions was, "Is this purchase really necessary?" I now ask myself that question every time I think about spending money—and doing this has truly changed my life. I have saved over $6,000 in six months and I have lost 21 pounds. David, you are a lifesaver, in more ways than one! Thank you for everything!

Nicole D.
Yuba City, CA

HOW THIS BOOK WORKS:
THE FINISH RICH PLAN TO ACHIEVE
FINANCIAL FREEDOM

We're going to start the process of achieving financial freedom by learning how to change your mindset, cut your expenses, and live within your means. Next, I'll shoe you how the credit card companies imprison you with tricks and traps in order to keep you in debt for life. Once you understand their games, you'll be able to fight back and win—and achieve real financial freedom.

Then we will look at what I call the DEBT FREE FOR LIFE MINDSET. This will help you get to the root of why you got into debt in the first place—and how you can get out of it once and for all.

Debt is often created because, without thinking about it, we spend money we don't have to buy things we were *subconsciously PROGRAMMED* to buy. Re-read that sentence! Companies spend BILLIONS AND BILLIONS of marketing dollars each and every year to bombard you with enticements to spend money. Trust me when I tell you that just about anyone can get out of debt once they become conscious of this. On the other hand, if your mindset on debt is wrong, you'll probably never get out of debt—and if you do, the odds are that you'll get right back in. That's not good enough. We want you DEBT FREE FOR LIFE!

YOUR DO-IT-YOURSELF SYSTEM—
THE DEBT FREE FOR LIFE TOOL KIT

Once we've got your DEBT FREE FOR LIFE MINDSET right, we'll look at my do-it-yourself system for getting out of debt. It's called DOLP®, which stands for "Done on Last Payment."

This is a simple system that I have taught for more a decade to prioritize your debt so you can pay it off as fast and cheaply as possible. One of the great things about DOLP is that you can do it from the comfort and safety of your own home with zero technology. All you need is a pen or pencil and a sheet or two of paper.

WHERE TO GO FOR HELP— WHO CAN YOU TRUST?

Although I believe that most of you who read this book should be able to implement the do-it-yourself systems I will teach you to reduce your debt, I know that some people would prefer to have the help of a professional who can personally help guide them through the process. If you're one of these people, don't worry. Once I've finished explaining the ins and outs of DOLP, I will share everything you need to know about how to find a qualified expert who can help you get out of debt.

As part of this process, I will explain in detail how the non-profit consumer credit counselling world works and what credit counsellors can do for you. We'll also explore the debt-settlement industry (the "for-profit" debt-reduction business) and what to watch out for, since this is a world filled with pitfalls. This is important for everyone to know, whether you plan to seek out counselling or not.

We will then cover the secrets to getting out of debt that the credit card companies don't want me to share, including how to get your interest rates lowered, your late fees waived, your annual fees credited back, and more. I will teach you how to negotiate for a better rate, and if you can't get a better deal on your current card, how to find a new one.

Along the way, I will share with you everything you need to know about your all-important credit score and credit reports. You'll learn how to protect and improve your score—which ultimately will make it easier to renegotiate your debt. And I will help you better understand your mortgage and student loans and what you can do to pay them off faster.

I will also cover bankruptcy (although I hope you never need this chapter) and share with you a ten-minute plan to put your entire financial life on Automatic Pilot (called The Automatic Millionaire System). Lastly, I will suggest some ways to find some extra money you may not have realized you have—money you could use to help you pay down your debt.

It's a lot to cover, but I have done my best to make it all easy to understand and—most importantly—to ACT ON.

As in many of my previous books, each chapter ends with a series of action steps—in this case, "Debt Free for Life Action Steps"—a condensed "to-do" list designed to remind you what you need to do and to help you keep track of your progress.

DEBT FREE FOR LIFE SUCCESS STORY

After reading *The Automatic Millionaire*, my first goal was to become debt-free within a year. So we started putting 20% of our family income toward paying off our debt. This limited our available money, but it was not a burden to us since we had decided to simplify our lives. We did this by cutting down on shopping, doing more meaningful activities, and driving our paid-off car longer instead of getting a new one with a consumer loan. Now, after only one year, we paid off all of our debt ($12,000), plus I was able to establish a four-month financial cushion for security. Before I read your book and worked your plan, I would have spent the "extra money"

I was earning from freelancing on all kinds of things, but now I am determined to act differently. This time I have goals. It has not been as hard as I expected. For the first time, our family doesn't have to live paycheque to paycheque. I can't wait to achieve the next goals on my list and to put more of your advice to work. Once again thank you very much!

Brigitte R.
Seattle, WA

THANK YOU FOR TRUSTING
THAT I MAY HAVE A PLAN FOR YOU!

Before we get started, let me once again say, THANK YOU! Many of you know me for my *New York Times* #1 bestsellers *The Automatic Millionaire* and *Start Late, Finish Rich*. Others may know me from my bestsellers *Smart Women Finish Rich, Smart Couples Finish Rich,* or last year's bestseller *Start Over, Finish Rich*. If you liked those books, I think you will LOVE this one. Many of you have written to me over the last few years and asked me to write a book like this. I hope it meets your expectations.

But whether you've read all my previous books or this is the first book of mine that you have picked up, I am truly grateful that we are getting to spend this time together, and I'm excited to have the chance to really help you deal with your debt. Together, I truly believe we can tackle the debt that is holding us back, and move each and every one of our lives forward powerfully.

DEBT FREE FOR LIFE ACTION STEPS

Reviewing what we discussed in this chapter, here is what you should be doing right now to become Debt Free for Life. Check off each step as you accomplish it.

❏ Recognize that we have let debt get out of control—and that as a result, we are in danger of losing once and for all our dream of financial freedom.

❏ Commit to taking action now to change your situation, reduce your debt, and become DEBT FREE FOR LIFE! Join the **"Debt Free Challenge"** at **www.finishrich.com**.

CHAPTER TWO

DEBT MATH:
HOW LENDERS KEEP YOU BROKE

Are you ready to learn more? Great—let's keep going. What I'm going to show you now is how the debt companies imprison you with basic math in order to keep you in debt for life. By learning their games, you'll be able to fight back and win— and achieve real financial freedom.

HOW TO GO BROKE ONE LOAN AT A TIME

What's amazing about debt is how easy it is to get into—and how hard it is to get out of if you don't understand the basic math. It's this math, which the debt companies understand— and we don't—that makes them rich and keeps us poor.

Let's just start with basic math of credit card debt.

- Let's say you borrow $5,000 on one of your credit cards.

- You get your bill; it says your interest rate is 19% and your minimum payment is $125.

- You make the minimum payments—and it takes you *25 years* to get out of debt.

- And it costs you $8,091.91 in interest charges.

Wow—is that really true? *How can it be?* I have posed this same question in my books for well over a decade now. How can credit card companies legally get away with not explaining this to their customers? It just doesn't seem right. You can go to a retailer and get a credit card in less than five minutes, not know the math, and wind up in debt for the rest of your life.

And this basic math assumes you will never purchase another thing on this card, never pay your bills late, never go over your credit limit, or pay any annual fees. If you do any of these things, it could take you years longer to get rid of that credit card debt. **And that's just one credit card!**

New credit card regulations announced in 2010 by the federal government finally force credit card companies to show us the truth about what I call the minimum payment scam. These regulations require credit card companies to note on your monthly statement the insanity of the minimum-payment math—specifically, how long it will take you to pay off your current balance and how much it will cost you if you make only minimum payments. Don't take my word for this—go look at your most recent credit card statement right now. The information should be there. If it's not, go online to **www.finishrich.com/debtcalculator** and run this calculation yourself. (And complain to your financial institution or credit card issuer; if this information is not spelled out on your monthly statement, your credit card company is violating federal regulations.)

HERE'S WHAT HAPPENS IF YOU ADD $10 A DAY

What I am about to show you will not be on your credit card statement. It should be, but it isn't. Let's take another look at the payment scenario I laid out above—but this time let's make one small change.

- You borrow $5,000 on one of your credit cards.

- You decide you don't want to spend 25 years paying this card off—you want to be out of debt sooner.

- **So you resolve that on top of the minimum payment, you will add $10 a day to pay down this debt (calculated as $300 a month).**

- If you do this, you would pay off this debt in—try this on for size—*14 months!*

- Your interest charges would total just $577.07 (vs. $8,091.91).

- **In other words, you could save more than $7,500 with this one simple tip.**

Honestly, isn't this math pretty stunning? I mean, really? How is it possible that it took decades for the government to start forcing the credit card companies to explain this to their customers—i.e. us. The reason is simple. Ignorance is profitable—just not for you. And by the way, if the interest rate on the example I just gave wasn't an outrageous 19% like millions of Canadians are now being forced to pay—and instead was the national average (which as I write this is 14%)—you would be out of debt with this one tip in less than 13 months and save 7,681.94.

NOW LET'S LOOK AT MORTGAGES

Here's the basic math for mortgage debt.

- You borrow $200,000 to buy a home.

- You get a 25-year fixed mortgage at 8% annual interest.

- Your monthly mortgage payment will be $1,526.43.

- The total cost of the mortgage over the 25-year life of the loan will be $457,926.12.

- **And the interest costs you $257,926.12!**

This mortgage math should be more familiar to you because the banks have long had to provide you with a mortgage amortization schedule when you sign your loan documents.

What they don't usually do is show you alternative payment plans. Let's look at what would happen if you added $10 a day toward your mortgage payment.

HERE'S WHAT HAPPENS IF YOU ADD $10 A DAY

- You borrow $200,000 to buy a home.

- You decide you really don't want to spend two and a half decades paying off your mortgage—you want to be out of debt sooner.

- **So you resolve to add $10 a day to your mortgage payment (calculated as $300 a month).**

- If you do this, you would pay off your mortgage in a little over 16 years!

- The total cost of your mortgage would be $353,833.66 (vs. $457,926.12).

- **In other words, you would save more than $104,000 with this one simple tip.**

I just gave you two incredibly simple examples of the basic arithmetic of debt. Simply by suggesting that you add $10 a day to your minimum required payment, I shaved nearly 24 years off what it would take to get rid of a $5,000 credit card debt. With an identical suggestion, I cut the time it would take to pay off a 25-year mortgage by more than a third.

Later on in this book, I will give you all kinds of tools to figure out breaks like these for yourself. But for now just let it settle in how much faster you can get out of debt by making small extra payments—in the correct way.

DEBT FREE FOR LIFE SUCCESS STORY

I am a single 32-year-old mom with an 11-year-old son. I read *Smart Women Finish Rich* a few years ago and got inspired to start taking control of my spending. I had a credit card for every store in the mall, karate tuition for my son, along with medical bills piling up. After I really applied your DOLP system, I really started to feel good. Since seeing you speak in NYC in 2006, I got motivated to start paying down my debt, and writing out my financial goals. Using your tools, I have managed to pay down $45,000 in credit card debt, paid off my son's karate tuition, and even saved for a down payment for a home. I just closed on my first condo this August, and cannot begin to tell you how excited I feel. Thank you for your inspiration and guidance you provide.

Joann G.
Hartford, CT

I COULD GO ON AND ON WITH THE MATH

By now, I'm sure you are getting the point. If these two examples left you thinking, "This is just nuts—if adding $10 a day to my minimum payments can get rid of a $5,000 credit card debt in little over a year and cut nine years off my home mortgage, I'm doing this!"—then congratulations! This tip alone will not only save you a fortune but also may make it possible for you to retire a decade earlier (regardless of what the stock market or the economy is doing).

Now here's the great news. This book will do a lot more than just show you how adding $10 a day to your payments can make you debt free. This book will give you an entire system to prioritize your debts so you can pay them off faster and more efficiently than you probably think is possible. You'll learn the tricks the debt industry doesn't want you to know.

The fact is that becoming debt free for life can be done, and in fact is being done. Throughout the book I'll offer a selection of remarkable stories of real people who used my Debt Free for Life Plan to get out of debt. If they can do it, you can

DEBT FREE FOR LIFE   29

do it. This book will be your road map—your tool kit for a life of financial freedom. *All you need to do is decide to get started.*

Are you getting excited? Good—then let's keep going. Your new plan—your new Debt Free for Life—awaits you.

A BONUS GIFT: The Latte Factor iPhone App

I know there will be some of you who may read this and think $10 a day is still a lot of money. I know it is—but I also know that most of you who are reading this can afford that and much more. The problem is that you're spending it on small things. For nearly two decades now, I have been talking about what I call the Latte Factor®. It's a phrase I coined to describe how wasting money on small things can have a huge impact on your finances, and it has gone around the world inspiring people to take charge of their financial lives. You can learn more about this online at **www.finishrich.com**. There are hundreds of Latte Factor Success Stories as well as a FREE Latte Factor iPhone app and calculator.

I hope this chapter has motivated you to stop falling for the minimum-payment scam. In fact, I truly hope that this month you do more than add $10 a day to your minimum payment—ideally, triple or quadruple it!

With that, let's take a look at your Debt Free for Life Mindset. Once we've got your thinking clear, we can get started on your action plan!

DEBT FREE FOR LIFE ACTION STEPS

❑ Pull out your most recent credit card statements and see how much it will cost you if you keep making minimum payments.

❑ Go to **www.finishrich.com** and see what would happen if you doubled the minimum payment on every one of your credit card balances

❑ Understand the minimum payment scam and resolve to stop falling for it.

CHAPTER THREE

THE DEBT FREE FOR LIFE MINDSET

You're ready to begin getting out of debt, aren't you? I'm sure you're motivated, and that's great—but motivation can wear off. If you want your motivation to stick, you need to be really clear about why you want to be out of debt. So our first goal is to make sure you truly understand why you want to be DEBT FREE FOR LIFE.

You may think the answer is obvious. But it's generally not what you think it is, and unless you really figure it out, you're not going to be able to get yourself out of debt for good.

How do you figure it out? By answering just seven questions—what I call the "DEBT FREE FOR LIFE QUESTIONS"—you can see whether or not you're really ready to make this journey.

WHY DO YOU REALLY WANT TO BE DEBT FREE FOR LIFE?

Before we start with the questions, let me share a little story. A few years ago, I was doing a series of shows with Oprah Winfrey called the "Debt Diet" series. What we were doing on these shows was creating a debt-reduction plan that millions of people could follow. And in fact millions of viewers who watched the shows took advantage of the online tools we created on Oprah.com and went on our Debt Diet.

After each show, we would have lunch with people selected from the audience to discuss their debt issues and what their challenges were. We wanted to better understand exactly what kind of help they needed, what they were learning, and what was working or not working for them.

At the end of one of these lunches, one of the couples we had picked came up to me. Both the husband and wife had broad grins on their faces. "We get it!" the wife announced happily.

I wasn't sure what she was talking about. "You get what?" I asked.

"We get why we really want to be out of debt," she explained. "At first, we were so focused on the details—the size of our payments, which credit card bill to pay first, that sort of thing. But then at lunch you asked us why we really want to be out of debt. We didn't have an answer—but now we do. We just decided. We both really want to be out of debt because we basically hate what we do for a living. Our daughter is disabled, and we want to be teachers who help kids like her—and if we get debt free, we can go for our dreams of teaching disabled kids. The thing is, it won't be enough for us to just pay down our credit cards. We will need to radically cut down our overhead and move to a less expensive community. But if we do that—and we know we can with your plan—then we can really go live our dreams. We just discussed it and we think we can do this in less than three years!"

Her husband broke in at this point. "This morning before the show we were discouraged about our debt and now we are totally excited!" he said. "This isn't really about our credit card debt—it's about what we really want our lives to be like. You helped us figure that out, David—and we're starting today. As soon as we get home. So thank you. You really did it for us."

I was thrilled for them. "Just remember," I said, "all I did was ask you the question. You found the answer. Good luck!"

And off they went to a new and more exciting life.

SEVEN BIG (BUT SIMPLE) QUESTIONS

So now let's go back to you. Imagine you are with me backstage at Oprah's studio, just like that couple. Or imagine you're at the beach with me right now (yes, I'm writing this at the beach in Del Mar, California—it's gorgeous, wish you were here).

I'm going to ask you seven simple questions about your debt. Don't get nervous. There are no RIGHT answers—only honest answers.

By the way, if you are married or in a committed long-term relationship where you share finances, you should discuss these questions with your partner. Don't assume that just because you love each other, you and your Significant Other share the same views on spending and debt. The number-one cause of divorce in this country isn't sex or religion or problems with the in-laws. It's disagreements over money, and more often than you might think those disagreements come as a total surprise to one or both parties. Having advised thousands of couples over the years, I can tell you from firsthand experience that working on your money together significantly improves the chances not only of your succeeding financially but of your staying together happily as a couple. So make this a joint effort.

Okay? Here goes:

- Why do you want to get out of debt—or be DEBT FREE FOR LIFE?

- Why are you in debt?

- How much debt do you have?

- What percentage of your income goes to pay interest charges on your debt?

- Who would you need to help you?

- What is the worst thing that could happen if you don't get out of debt?

- When will you start?

Easy questions, right? Now let's answer them—as honestly as you can.

QUESTION ONE:
WHY DO YOU WANT TO BE DEBT FREE FOR LIFE?

I want to be debt free for life because ...

Let's look at your answer. Does it feel honest to you? Does it feel really meaningful? Does it excite you? Can you taste or feel the outcome? Is it vivid—or does it need more details?

I'll give you an example. You could write, "I'm carrying $10,000 in credit card debt, and it stresses me out, and I'm worried every month when the bills come. I'm paying 19% in annual interest, and I feel stupid wasting this money—so the faster I pay it down, the better. I know when I pay it off I will feel GREAT."

That was a simple example, but you get the gist.

Then again, your answer could be much more vivid and deeper. You might read that question and come up with a deeply personal spiritual reason. I remember when I asked this question at a seminar I once gave, a reader named Richard choked up and nearly burst into tears. "My entire life I have been afraid of being homeless, being left in the street with nothing," he said. "My father was an alcoholic who walked out on us when I was six. My mom and I and my brother and sister were left penniless. We ended up on the streets, living with crack addicts, then in homeless shelters. For years, we went to bed hungry. I never felt safe. The kids at school made fun of me because of my beat-up clothes and because I smelled. I'm afraid every day that this could happen again."

Richard paused for a moment, then continued. "I want to know that I will never be homeless again. That my savings will always be safe, and that I won't need to depend on anyone. I also want my two kids to always be safe from financial worry and I would like to help them someday buy a home. The sooner I pay down my mortgage, the sooner I feel like I can focus on building up a trust to help them someday buy their own homes. Helping my kids own a home feels like the greatest gift I could give them other than my unconditional love. Knowing I am working towards these goals will give me peace of mind, and achieving them I believe will bring me serenity. I feel better just imagining it happen right now."

So again, I ask you:

Why do you want to be DEBT FREE FOR LIFE?

Write your answer in the space provided above or on a piece of paper or in your journal, if you have one (I hope you do). If you're married or in a relationship, do this exercise with your partner. This journey towards becoming Debt Free for Life is a really great one to go on together.

Having this conversation with yourself and the ones you love can help you go from being fearful to being hopeful. (And don't worry if right now you don't know how you will get there. That part will come later.)

> ## QUESTION TWO:
> ## WHY ARE YOU IN DEBT?

My goal with this question is not to have you beat yourself up, but rather to have you face the truth about how you got where you are today. Did something tragic happen, like a medical problem? Did you lose a job? Did you buy a bigger house than you could afford? Did you live beyond your means?

What really happened? You may not be living paycheque to paycheque, but are simply carrying more debt than you are comfortable with. How did you get there?

Just answer the question from your heart as honestly as you can.

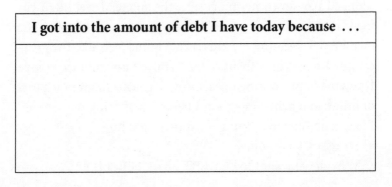

I got into the amount of debt I have today because . . .

QUESTION THREE:
HOW MUCH DEBT DO YOU HAVE?

In the next chapter, we will cover exactly how to determine how much debt you have, and I'll provide you with worksheets to help you do this. For now, just make an educated guess. How much debt do you have that you want to pay off? Go ahead and just write it down now.

I estimate that my total debt (house, cars, student loans, credit cards—you name it) as of [insert today's date] _____ is $_____.

QUESTION FOUR:
WHAT PERCENTAGE OF YOUR INCOME GOES TO PAY INTEREST CHARGES ON YOUR DEBT?

This is probably not a question you can answer right now. More than likely, you'll need to come back to this one after you read the next chapter. But it may be the most eye-opening question of the seven. What I want you to do is pull out your mortgage statement, your car loan statement, your student loan statement, your credit card statement—the most recent statement for every loan you have—and figure out exactly how much of your monthly payment goes to interest charges. For example, say your mortgage payment is $2,000 a month. Chances are that less than $150 of that goes toward paying down the principal. The rest is going to interest. The same is true for your credit card bill. If you make a minimum payment of $200 a month on a credit card bill, most likely all but maybe $25 of that is eaten up by interest charges. In order to know where you really stand, you need to break out how much of your debt payments go to interest and how much to principal.

This may involve calling your lenders and asking them to give you the facts. And the answers may shock you. Once you add up all the interest you are paying, you may find that more than half your take-home pay is going right into the lenders' pockets—without helping you make one inch of financial progress. Remember, the only time you get ahead with debt is when you pay down principal. This is why so many people (maybe you're one of them) complain about paying so much on their loans—and never seeing the balances shrink. Frustrating, right? It's why you need to know what proportion of your take-home pay is going toward paying interest charges.

My *total interest payments*
each month are: $_____
My take-home pay each
month is: $_____
The proportion of my take-home
pay that goes to pay interest
charges is: _____%
(divide your interest payments by your
take-home pay to get answer above)

QUESTION FIVE:
WHO CAN HELP YOU GET OUT OF DEBT?

Now I want you to think about who you may need to turn to in order to help you get out of debt. This book is designed for you to be able to do it yourself—meaning that, if you follow the plan I lay out and use the tools I provide, you should be able to get yourself out of debt. That said, maybe you're not the do-it-yourself type. Maybe you feel you'll need a professional credit counsellor to help guide you through the process. If that's true for you, then great—write it down. And even if doing it yourself is not a problem for you, if you have a family, you are going to need their help and support to get out of debt. Trust me—it's really hard to get out of debt if the people around you are spending you back into it. So if you have a spouse and/or kids, you may want to add them to your answer here. Also, you should definitely add me to your list—because I am committed to helping you. (Along those lines, aside from reading this book, the first thing you can do towards letting me help you is to get my DEBT FREE FOR LIFE VIDEO SERIES, which is free for you at **www.finishrich.com**.)

I have decided that the following people will help me to get out of debt:

QUESTION SIX:
WHAT'S THE WORST THING THAT COULD HAPPEN IF YOU DON'T GET OUT OF DEBT?

I include this question because it's important that you face your fear about debt. Being in debt is an everyday thing. Debt is always with you. You have it right now. So my question to you is really simple: what will your life look like in the future if you *don't* deal with your debt?

Facing your fear about your debt is not being pessimistic—it's being honest. And the more honest you are right now, the better. So tell yourself the truth. Write down what your worst-case scenario could be.

In fact, once you write out your worst fear, you will more than likely realize it isn't going to happen—and just realizing that will make you feel better. And if you really believe the worst could happen, then writing it out will motivate you even more to act quickly and decisively to start dealing with your debt.

> **The worst thing that could happen if I don't deal with my debt is . . .**

QUESTION SEVEN:
WHEN WILL YOU START?

Below you will find the "Debt Free for Life Pledge," which I've created to mark your new commitment to leading a debt-free life. By signing it, you are making a promise not to me but to yourself and your loved ones—a promise that you are truly headed toward a new life of financial freedom. I hope you will consider that reading this book means you have already started the process of becoming debt free for life. If you do, you should sign the pledge and put down today's date. It will be nice when you celebrate your Debt Freedom Day to pull this paper out and see in your own handwriting the promise you made on the day you started to change your life.

NOW TAKE AND SIGN THE
DEBT FREE FOR LIFE PLEDGE

I _____[insert your name] commit to be out of debt by _____ [insert date].

I believe that paying down my debt and being DEBT FREE FOR LIFE is critically important, and I am ready to work to make it happen.

I will start my journey to being out of debt on _____ [insert date].

Signed _____

DEBT FREE FOR LIFE SUCCESS STORY

In August of 2007, I read an article you wrote on Yahoo Finance about your DOLP method of paying off your credit cards. At the time, I had $46,000 in credit card debt and didn't believe I could ever get out from under it. Now it's August of 2010 and we are down to two credit cards and our debt is down to $12,000! One of those cards will be paid off in a matter of months, and I expect to be completely debt free by next year. I can finally see the light at the end of the tunnel. Not only that, but we are living within our means and have some savings (no small feat these days). Thank you for your rational and systematic approach. You have made a real difference in our lives.

Phil L.
Santa Cruz, CA

TAKE THE PLEDGE AND WIN

Now go to **www.finishrich.com** or **www.facebook.com/davidbach** and take the "Debt Free Pledge" online. Show publicly that you are ready to be Debt Free for LIFE! And share this with your friends and loved ones. Let's start a movement together!

You can also join our Debt Free Challenge and win online goodies for signing up and earn prizes as you stay on your plan. All details are on the Debt Free Life Challenge website, which you will find at **www.finishrich.com**.

THINKING IS OFTEN THE HARDEST THING TO DO— AND YOU JUST DID IT!

Congratulations on taking the time to read my questions and answer them. Even if you haven't stopped reading and started writing, the fact that you asked the questions of yourself means you have started the process. And if you *have* taken the time to write the answers (as I hope you did—or will do), then well done! I'm proud of you. Now let's get started on my do-it-yourself system for getting out of debt. As I said earlier, all you need is a pen or pencil, a sheet or two of paper—and the desire to be Debt Free for Life.

DEBT FREE FOR LIFE ACTION STEPS

❏ Ask yourself the seven Debt Free for Life Mindset questions—and answer them as honestly as you can.
❏ Take and sign the Debt Free for Life pledge at **www.finishrich.com.**
❏ Go online and share your pledge publicly.

CHAPTER FOUR

IF YOU'RE IN A HOLE, STOP DIGGING

You just answered the seven questions about why you want to be out of debt—and you've got your Debt Free for Life Mindset started! Well done. Now before we jump into the "how to crush your debt" portion of this book, I want to mention one absolutely vital idea you need to understand and accept if you are going to have any chance of becoming debt free for life. It's the kind of thing that you might think goes without saying, and to be honest I debated with myself about whether or not to include it here. In the end, I figured it couldn't hurt. So here goes.

A big part of getting out of debt is realizing that when you are in a hole, you have to stop digging. This is one of the great truths of achieving financial freedom: you can't become debt free if you keep piling on the debt. Too often I meet people who do a great job of paying down one credit card, only to start piling up debt on a new credit card the moment they get a "special offer" in the mail. Or I meet someone who tells me that they've just paid off their car—and then six months later, they are driving a brand new car with a new lease payment! Or they get close to paying off their mortgage, and then refinance, lowering their payments but stretching out the term of their debt. Hello! The point here is to get your debt paid off for good!

HOW MY CREDIT CARDS
WOUND UP IN THE MICROWAVE

When I share the idea that when you are in a debt hole you need to stop digging, I'm speaking from experience. You see, back when I was in college, I had huge problems with spending in general and credit cards in particular. By the beginning of my senior year, I owed more than ten thousand dollars in credit card debt. I had three cards and was desperate to get them paid off, but nothing seemed to work for me. I tried everything—all the stupid tricks—even the dumb one where you put your credit cards in a bowl of water and freeze them, so if you're tempted to use them, you have to wait for the ice to melt.

Of course, what happened was that some friends organized a spur-of-the-moment trip to Las Vegas and naturally I had to go with them. They were in a big hurry, so instead of waiting for the ice to melt, I put the bowl in the microwave—and guess what happened?

I melted my credit cards.

I swear this is true. I'm laughing as I type this because it's so dumb. I also tried the trick where you leave your credit cards in your car when you go shopping. All this did was make me get all hot and sweaty when I went running back to my car to retrieve them. Cutting up my cards didn't work either. When my cards expired, the card companies sent me new ones. I couldn't help myself—I activated them and went back to charging up a storm.

If this sounds like the behaviour of an addict—well, that's what it was. In college, credit cards were like a drug for me. I literally couldn't stop using them.

What changed? One day the bills arrived in the mail and I was too afraid to open the envelopes. I finally opened them with my eyes closed and my heart racing. When I managed to open my eyes and saw the numbers inside, I almost got sick. How had I done this to myself? This was INSANE.

That was the day I woke up to the truth. The truth was that I was spending money I didn't have to buy things I didn't need. None of the things I was buying were "life necessary." I was rationalizing my overspending. I wanted to be out of debt and the only way I would ever get there was to STOP SPENDING MONEY.

MY GRANDMA ROSE SET ME STRAIGHT

Around this time, I went to see my grandmother Rose Bach. Grandma Rose had always been one of my money mentors, and I told her all about how stressed I was about my credit card debt. To be honest, I was half hoping she would help me out. Instead of giving me money, however, she gave me advice.

"David," she said, "you want to be rich someday, true?"

"Yes, Grandma," I replied. "I want to be a millionaire by the time I'm 30."

"Well, then," she said, "let me give you some simple advice. You can't out-earn your debt."

I must have looked puzzled, because she smiled and said, "There are rich people every day going broke and there are middle-class people getting rich. Your grandmother is an example of a self-made middle-class woman who became a millionaire because she saved money, she invested—and, above all, she never, ever spent money on anything if she couldn't afford to pay cash for it." She looked at me sternly. "David, you are a smart guy, but you need to grow up. You're about to graduate from college. My advice to you is knock it off. Stop spending money you don't have. Cut up your credit cards for good, pay them off—and never go back. When you get out of college live like you are poor—so in ten years you can actually be rich. Remember: it's not how much you make that will determine whether or not you become wealthy. *It's how much you spend.*"

I LISTENED TO MY GRANDMA— YOU SHOULD TOO

Grandma Rose always knew how to get through to me. For the rest of my time in college, I stopped using my credit cards. In fact, it took me nearly two full years to pay off all of my credit card debt. And from then on, I used only a debit card and a single charge card (one that did not allow me to carry a balance but rather required me to pay it off in full every month). I'm now in my forties, and this method has worked for me for more than two decades now. I have not had any credit card debt since my early twenties.

Equally if not more important, I have also constantly tried to spend less than I earn. What my grandmother made me realize was that debt reduction equals wealth. I can't tell you I did this all perfectly. I have shared in other books how I also leased a fancy car at a young age and rented an apartment. But Grandma Rose's lecture never left me—and I did become a millionaire by the age of 30.

The basic lesson that my grandmother drilled into my head was, as she said, a simple one—and it's one I want you to think about (and discuss with your spouse or partner if you are married or in a committed relationship where you share finances): The only way out of a debt hole is to stop digging.

Okay—enough sermonizing. Now let's get started on my do-it-yourself system for getting out of debt. As I said earlier, all you need is a pen or pencil, a sheet or two of paper—and the desire to be Debt Free for Life.

DEBT FREE FOR LIFE ACTION STEPS

❑ Acknowledge that you can't become debt free if you keep piling on debt.

❑ Stop spending money you don't have on things you don't need.

❑ Try to spend less than you earn.

CHAPTER FIVE

THE DOLP® METHOD:
HOW TO PAY DOWN YOUR DEBT
IN RECORD TIME

So you're ready to get going, aren't you? Good, because now I'm going to share with you a system to pay off your debts that is so simple you can be up and running with it in less than an hour.

Yes, you read that correctly! If you follow the instructions I am about to lay out for you, in less than one hour you will have a foolproof system to pay off everything you owe once and for all.

The system is called DOLP®, short for Done On Last Payment. (In my previous books, I wrote that DOLP stood for "Dead On Last Payment," but readers suggested that "Done" was more motivating than "Dead"—so I have changed it). The DOLP system is the cornerstone of your Debt Free for Life Plan. I've been talking about DOLP for well over a decade now. I've taught it to millions of people on shows like *Oprah* and NBC's *Today*, and through numerous appearances on ABC, CBS, Fox, and other TV networks. I've also described it in a few of my previous books. There's a good reason I've stuck with the DOLP system all these years: it's simple and *it works*.

Are you ready? Great—let's go.

GET STARTED ORGANIZING YOUR DEBT

The first step in DOLPing your way out of debt is to get organized. It's a lot like getting on a scale before you start a diet. You have to step right up, open your eyes, look down—and face the truth.

Debt is something you need to see in black and white. You can't expect your Debt Free for Life Plan to work—and you won't be able to measure your progress each month as you pay down your debt—unless you start off knowing exactly how much you owe.

Are you excited? You should be. You're about to change your whole life.

GO GET YOUR CREDIT CARD STATEMENTS

To start the process of getting your debt organized, the first thing you need to do is go and get all the statements and other documents from every credit card account you have. Then go and get some folders. (Ideally, they should be red so they will stand out in your file drawer.) Now create a file for each different credit card account and label it appropriately (e.g., "Visa Credit Card"). From now on, you will put all of your statements and payment receipts for this particular account in this particular folder.

On the front of each folder, I want you to write with a big black marker the total amount of debt you currently owe on each card. Make the numbers big and bold so you can instantly see in black and white how big this particular debt is, and next to this figure write down today's date. Each time you make a payment that reduces this credit card debt, you will cross out the old total and below it write down the new, smaller total you owe.

In this way, you will automatically create a handwritten

journal that keeps track of how your debt is shrinking. Just seeing a record—*in your own handwriting*—of the progress you are making each month is going to motivate you as never before.

In a few minutes, you are going to take this information about your credit card debt and start filling out the DOLP Worksheet on page 58. But for now I simply want you to do the simple arithmetic needed to complete the short credit card worksheet below.

FIGURE OUT HOW MANY
CREDIT CARDS YOU HAVE

Number of credit cards I have: _____

Number of credit cards my
spouse/partner has: _____

Number of credit cards my kids
(or other dependents) have: _____

Total number of credit cards
my whole family has: _____

The total amount of debt we
carry on these credit cards is $_____

The total monthly
minimum payment due is $_____

To figure out the totals, use the worksheet below. List each credit card account and its current outstanding balance, starting with the smallest debt and working down to the largest. In this way you will figure out exactly how much you owe and who you owe it to.

DEBT REALITY WORKSHEET				
Name of Creditor	Account Number	Outstanding Balance	Monthly Minimum Payment	Interest Rate
1.				
2.				
3.				
4.				
5.				
6.				
7.				
8.				
9.				
10.				
11.				
12.				
13.				

NOW FIGURE OUT ALL YOUR OTHER DEBTS

Once you've filed all your credit card statements and added up your totals, it's time to add up all the other debt you have—mortgages, car loans, student loans, lines of credit, everything. To begin with, I want you to gather up all the statements for your mortgage and related debts, such as second (or third) mortgages and home equity loans. As you did before, create a file for each debt, label it (e.g., "Scotiabank home mortgage"), and on the front of the folder write the total amount you currently owe. Do the same for any car loans or other personal loans you may have. Finally, if you still owe money on a student loan, make a file and write the total current loan balance on the front of the folder.

Now add up all of this other debt and record it as follows.

I owe $_____ on my primary mortgage.
I owe $_____ on second mortgages/home equity loans, etc.
I owe $_____ on second property/vacation homes or rental properties.
I owe $_____ on student loans.
I owe $_____ on car loans/boat loans.
I owe $_____ on other installment debt.

The total amount of additional debt I carry is $_____.

The Grand Total I owe as of _____ [today's date] is $_____.

ADDING UP ALL OF YOUR DEBT ISN'T FUN— BUT IT IS HELPFUL

I'm not going to pretend that what I have just asked you to do won't hurt. Having coached literally thousands of people on this process, I can't tell you the number of times I have seen someone almost go into shock when he sees in black and white how much he really owes and to how many different banks and companies. For many people, completing this exercise is the first time they've ever taken a good look at how deep in debt they actually are.

I once went through this process with a couple on a television show, and they were stunned to discover that they owed nearly twice what they had "guesstimated." They went on the show thinking they had about $40,000 in debt. In fact, the total turned out to be $72,000. I'll never forget the look on their faces when I showed them the final figure.

It was not a pleasant experience for them. But here's the reality of the situation—**you can't cure what you don't face.** The number-one mistake I see people making with their debt is what I call "debt denial." There's a dangerous attitude many of us have that can be summed up in the phrase: "If I don't see it, it's not real."

This is why so many people who are behind on debt payments don't even bother to open up the envelopes when their statements arrive in the mail. I'm sure this isn't you—but I am also willing to bet that you don't know exactly how much debt you currently have. Which is why this step, as simple as it is, is so critical.

> ## DEBT FREE FOR LIFE SUCCESS STORY
>
> David, I didn't really think it was possible. Getting out of debt is a bit like going on a diet. You try to get a handle on your finances, but you always slip back into old habits. It's been less than four years since I read *The Automatic Millionaire*, and I am proud to share that I am now DEBT FREE! I could not have done it without you. I bought the audio CDs to *Start Late, Finish Rich* and every time I got discouraged, I tossed a CD in the player and listened to it again and again. I have made so many financial changes in my life, but the most startling was using your system to get out of debt. You see, I have been carrying the same old debt for almost 30 years (that's not an exaggeration) and I can't tell you how incredible it feels to be rid of it. Now, all of that money that was going to pay interest on "things gone by" is being used to go into savings. Thank you David!
>
> **Pamela B.**
> **Coventry, CT**

LET'S ROLL UP OUR SLEEVES
AND BE HONEST WITH OURSELVES

According to the Canadian Bankers Association, there are two credit cards in circulation for every man, woman, and child in Canada. More than a quarter of the people who hold those 68 million cards do not pay them off from one month to the next. Among those people, the average balance on their cards is $2,000. That's just the average. In my experience as a money coach for nearly two decades, I have seen firsthand that when it comes to credit cards many of us operate way, way above average. Both on Oprah's "Debt Diet" series and on the weekly "Money 911" segments I did for *Today*, I have met and worked with people who had run up $25,000, $50,000, $75,000—even more than $100,000—in credit card debt.

There's a classic twist on the old song that the Seven Dwarfs sang in Disney's *Snow White*: "I owe, I owe—it's off to work I go." It's a cute line, but is that really what you want? I don't think so. In fact, I know you don't. If you did, you wouldn't be reading this book. So let's roll up our sleeves, be honest with ourselves and deal once and for all with how much debt we really have.

Use the Debt Reality Worksheet to total everything up.

DOLPING YOUR WAY OUT OF DEBT

Now that your debt is organized and you have all of your records in front of you, it's time to fill out the DOLP Worksheet. As I told you earlier, the DOLP system is the method I have taught for more than a decade to help people create an action plan that will get them out of debt. The process is simple, straightforward, and can be completed in less than an hour. In fact, if you have already done all the chores I said you needed to do up to this point, then you are pretty much done with the bulk of the work involved in creating a DOLP plan. All you really need to do now to get your "fast-pay plan" on paper is simply plug in your debt numbers.

The entire purpose of the DOLP plan is to build what I call debt-reduction momentum. In particular, it's about getting your credit card accounts paid down and "gone." By gone, I mean you have paid the cards off—and, ideally, have stopped carrying any debt on them. This is what I mean when I say you are going to DOLP your debts away—you are going to make sure your credit card and other loan accounts are Done on Last Payment. (I don't mean you should close the accounts. As you will see in

Chapter Seven when I discuss your credit score, you should probably keep them open to keep your credit score up.)

So here's how you do it.

1. Fill out the DOLP Worksheet.

Your DOLP Worksheet will become the "scale" that you will use to track how much total debt all your various loans add up to—and in which order you should pay them off. You'll find both a blank worksheet and a sample worksheet on pages 58-59. In addition, there's an interactive version online at **www.finishrich.com/dolp**. Whichever one you use, filling it out is really easy. In the first column, you simply write in the name of the loan account. In the next column, you put the balance you owe, followed by the minimum payment due. The fourth column is for the payment due date. For the moment, hold off on filling this in. The last two columns are for the loan's DOLP Number and its DOLP Ranking. These two items are the heart of the DOLP system, and figuring them out (which we'll do next) is super easy.

DOLP® WORKSHEET					
Account	Outstanding Balance	Minimum Monthly Payment	Payment Due Date	DOLP Number (Balance/Min Payment)	DOLP Ranking

SAMPLE DOLP WORKSHEET					
Account	Outstanding Balance	Minimum Monthly Payment	Payment Due Date	DOLP Number (Balance/Min Payment)	DOLP Ranking
Visa	$500	$50	10th of the month	10	1
MasterCard	$775	$65	15th of the month	12	2
HBC Credit Card	$1,150	$35	1st of the month	39	3

2. Calculate the DOLP Number for each account.

To figure out each account's DOLP number, you simply divide the outstanding balance by the minimum monthly payment. For example, if you owe $500 on your Visa card and your minimum payment is $50, you take the $500 and divide it by $50, which gives your Visa account a DOLP number of 10. The 10 represents how many monthly minimum payments (not counting interest) it would take to pay off your debt. After you've finished calculating a DOLP Number for all of your credit card accounts, do the same for your other debts. Keep in mind that with most closed-end loans, such as home mortgages, student loans, or car loans, you can find the number of payments left listed on your statements. If it's not there, leave the space for the DOLP Number blank. We'll come back to them later.

3. Assign each account a DOLP Ranking.

This is even easier than calculating the DOLP Number. The account with the lowest DOLP Number is ranked #1, the account with the second lowest is ranked #2, and so on. The table above shows you an example of how this might look.

4. Calendar your due dates.

Now I want you to fill in the "payment due date" column in the worksheet for all of your loans, credit card and otherwise. While you are at it, I also want you to add these due dates to whatever calendar system you use—whether it's on your computer (like Microsoft Outlook) or online (like Google Calendar) or on your desk (like an old-fashioned Day-at-a-Glance diary). Regardless of the technology involved, set your calendar to remind you of all your payment due dates at least five days ahead of time. This should prevent you from making any late payments—and thus making your situation even worse by getting hit with costly late fees. You can protect yourself even more by signing up with your credit card companies to receive an email alert when your bill arrives in your online banking mailbox. Also, once you've got all your due dates written down right in front of you, it's really easy to figure out how you might rearrange them so they come at the most convenient time for you (whether that's all at once or bunched twice a month). Most credit card companies and many other lenders will work with you to change their due dates for this very reason.

5. Fast-pay your debt—the DOLP way.

Now that your DOLP Worksheet is completely filled out, you're ready to start DOLPing your way out of debt. What the DOLP system does is tell you which of your loans you should pay off first in order to become debt-free as quickly as possible. Here's what you do. Each month, you make the minimum payment on every credit card account you have . . . EXCEPT the one with the lowest DOLP Ranking. For that card, you make as big a payment as you can manage. Ideally, this payment should be at least **double** the minimum payment. Using the examples in the sample worksheet on page 59, you would pay $65 to MasterCard, $35 to HBC, and at least $100 to Visa. Once a card has been paid off completely (you've DOLPed it—it's dead—hooray!), you bury it (which is to say you put it in a drawer, cut it up, etc.), and start attacking the account with the next lowest DOLP Ranking—in the example on page 59, the MasterCard.

THE DOLP SYSTEM: A PROVEN STRATEGY TO PAY DOWN DEBT

By creating a DOLP list of your debts, you now know which of your credit cards can and should be paid off fastest! The DOLP system works because it helps you quickly identify the card you can realistically pay off with the fewest payments. And once that card is paid off, you can put that much more toward paying off the card with the next-highest DOLP ranking. As each card is paid off, you have more money left to pay off your remaining cards. Seems easy, right? The truth is that the system *is* easy. It's simply a matter of prioritizing your debts and then fast-paying the right card down.

One question I am often asked is how much more than the minimum payment you should make to the card with the lowest DOLP Ranking. As I said earlier, I recommend paying at least twice the minimum payment—but more is always better because more means you will get the card paid off faster. And take it from me, if you haven't already experienced this yourself, there is nothing like the feeling you get when you check off a debt as paid in full. Hopefully, it won't be too long before you've got your #1 DOLP card paid off and you can start making extra payments on your #2 DOLP card. I have coached people who, in less than a year, were able to pay off more than a half-dozen credit card balances. Each time they retired a card, they celebrated (inexpensively).

That said, you shouldn't be under any illusions. DOLPing takes time, effort, and commitment. You've got to be realistic about this. It probably took you years to get into debt, so don't expect that you'll be able to get out of it in a few months. Several years is a more likely timeframe. But don't be discouraged. Your progress may be slower than you'd like, but with your newfound knowledge, a plan, and the will to take action, it will be steady.

WHY IT'S SO IMPORTANT TO REDUCE THE NUMBER OF CARDS YOU HAVE

The point of DOLPING your debt is to *reduce the number of credit card balances you are carrying—fast.* Using this method achieves this goal much faster than, say, focusing on the highest interest rate.

Reducing the number of different credit card debts you have is MISSION NUMBER ONE. Why? Because the more balances you carry, the greater the chance that you will be late on a payment or go over a credit limit—and get hit with huge penalty fees. Penalty fees are the bread and butter of the credit card industry. In many cases, credit card companies make more money from penalty and administrative fees than from interest charges. The fact is that a small card with even a small balance can cost you an absolute fortune. If you miss a payment on your "small card" with a $500 balance, the late fee could be as much as $50. If you keep using that card (and, again, you're not going to, right?) and you go over your credit limit, the penalty fee could be $100. Imagine—if you were late and went over the limit, the fee for the month would be $150!

This is why, when it comes to getting out of debt fast, there are more important factors than interest rates. And, by the way, the credit card companies built their business on this exact premise.

DEBT FREE FOR LIFE ACTION STEPS

❑ Create a file system for all your credit card accounts.
❑ Use the Debt Reality Worksheet to figure out how much debt you have and who you owe it to.
❑ Fill out the DOLP Worksheet and use the information in it to prioritize your debts by DOLP Number or use the free online DOLP worksheet at **www.finishrich.com/dolp**
❑ Start fast-paying your debts the DOLP way.

CHAPTER SIX

NEGOTIATE YOUR DEBT DOWN: HOW TO LOWER THE INTEREST RATES ON YOUR CREDIT CARDS

I want you to stop now and take a moment to recognize how far you've come in your Debt Free for Life Plan. You've faced up to your debt, organized it, prioritized it, and learned the math that the credit card companies don't want you to understand. In a short period of time, you've truly come a long way in dealing with your debt.

It's really important that you give yourself credit for the work you have done. Remember, *you* bought this book—*you* opened it, *you* have been reading it. You are doing the work and soul searching it takes to make better decisions about your future and your money. YOU ARE DEALING with your debt.

I'm not trying to make a "rah-rah" speech here. I'm reminding you of this because dealing with your debt is a lot like exercise. You don't get in shape overnight. It's easy to start anything, but the secret to success is not just starting—it's staying with it.

In this chapter, I'm going to share with you a five-step plan to lower the interest rates on your credit cards. While the steps themselves are incredibly simple, I want you to know upfront that none of this is a "slam dunk." It used to be much easier to get your credit card rates lowered than it is today. Once upon a time, just threatening to close your account would get a credit card company to give you a better rate. (I actually talked about this in my previous books.) But today, as a result of the recession, the debt meltdown, and the credit crunch, we are living in a different world. It used to be that higher rates were the penalty you paid for being a late payer or having a bad credit card score. But now, for no reason at all, credit card companies are hiking the interest rates they charge even long-time customers. They are also cutting credit limits and closing the accounts of cardholders who don't use them often enough.

Still, I don't want you to be discouraged. Even though the companies are fighting hard to keep interest rates high, people I coach do manage to get their rates lowered every day, and you can too. It will take work, but trust me—it will be worth it.

THE MATH BEHIND HIGH INTEREST RATES—
HOW THE CREDIT CARD COMPANIES GET YOU

The basic math of credit card interest rates is staggering. Consider what happened recently to a good friend of mine. Alice and I literally grew up together, and she has been reading my books for years. (It helps that I always give her a free copy.) Not long ago, when I gave her a copy of my last book, she had a story for *me*. "David," she said, "you won't believe what just happened to me with my Visa card."

The truth is nothing surprises me anymore when it comes to how low the credit card companies will stoop, but Alice's story actually did shock me. (To be honest, I was a little skeptical of her story until I checked it out myself.)

Here's what happened. Alice had been a loyal and responsible user of her Visa card since 1998. She loved the card because it enabled her to earn so many frequent-flyer points, and she always made her payments on time. While she normally paid off her monthly bill in full, she had recently lost her job and as a result she was currently carrying a balance of about $10,000. Her interest rate had always been rather low—about 9%—but following the advice I gave in my last book, *Start Over, Finish Rich,* she made a point of checking her statement to see what her current rate was. To her shock, she discovered that her bank was charging her 29%!

"Twenty-nine percent!" she thought. "That can't be. I've never once missed a payment. It must be a mistake."

So she called the phone number on her credit cart and asked if the figure she had seen on her statement was in fact correct. Was her rate really 29% or had she misread it?

The customer-service representative who took her call explained that, no, she hadn't misread it. Her rate *was* 29%.

Alice asked how that could be, and the nice customer service person explained that the bank had raised *everyone's* rates to 29%, regardless of their payment record or credit history.

When she got off the phone, Alice did the math. Here's what it looked like.

Alice's Visa card

$10,000 (interest rate 9%)
Total cost to pay off with 2.5% minimum payment: $14,192

$10,000 (interest rate 29%)
Total cost to pay off with 2.5% minimum payment: $85,547

AT 29% INTEREST, THERE IS A $71,355 DIFFERENCE!

Outrageous, right? Not surprisingly, Alice was mad, really mad.

"How can they do that?" she asked me. "And what can I do?"

While not everyone's situation is as difficult as Alice's, what she went through is similar to what millions of people are going through right now. Maybe you are one of them.

I told Alice to bring me her statement and we would call the credit card company together to see what could be done to negotiate her rate down.

Over the next several pages, I am going to share with you what Alice and I did, so you can do exactly the same thing for yourself. Keep in mind that Alice did not achieve instant success in getting her rates lowered. However, she did ultimately make progress, and so can you.

GET YOUR CREDIT CARD COMPANY TO GIVE YOU A BETTER RATE

The process of getting your interest rates lowered begins with your filling out the Debt Free for Life Negotiator Worksheet on page 69. You will use this worksheet to track the calls—and the progress—you make in negotiating your interest rate down. But before you do anything, I want you to read this section first in its entirety. Then fill out the worksheet and start making calls.

1. Find out how much interest you are paying

The first thing Alice did was to note the interest rate she was being charged on her credit card debts. If you filled out the DOLP Worksheet on page 58, you already have this information. If not, go get your latest credit card statements. Your APR, or Annualized Percentage Rate, should be listed at the very top or the very bottom of the statement. If you can't find it or, like Alice, you aren't sure you're reading it right, then call your credit card company and ask them what your APR is.

THE DEBT FREE FOR LIFE NEGOTIATOR WORKSHEET
My Current Credit Card Companies

Company	Balance	Current rate	Spoke to:	Offer	Staying/ Going?

New Companies I've Called

Company	What they offered	Accepting/Declining?

My Credit Cards and Rates Going Forward

Credit card #1
Old company _____   New company _____
Old rate _____%   New rate _____%

Credit card #2
Old company _____   New company _____
Old rate _____%   New rate _____%

Credit card #3
Old company _____   New company _____
Old rate _____%   New rate _____%

Credit card #4
Old company _____   New company _____
Old rate _____%   New rate _____%

2. Shop for a lower rate

The second thing I did with Alice was to have her "Google" all her credit cards (using each card's exact name) and compare the interest rate she was currently paying to the rate each of her card companies was offering to new customers. You should do the same thing now with all of your cards. In Alice's case, we were able to find out in less than five seconds that her bank was offering new Visa customers who qualified an APR of just 13%, *plus* 30,000 frequent-flyer miles once they charged $750. This is what you call adding insult to injury. Alice had been a Visa gold card customer for more than a decade, she had never been late making a payment, and she had a good credit score. Yet her bank had stuck her with an interest rate almost twice as high as what it was offering new customers. This is the type of information you want to know before you get on the phone to ask your credit card company for a lower rate.

3. Compare your rate to national averages

The beauty of the Internet is how easy it is to shop for interest rates—and to find out if you are being treated fairly. Yet very few people take advantage of this fact. You can get the latest credit card rates, along with national averages, at websites like **www.fcac-acfc.gc.ca**, **www.creditcards.ca**, **redflagdeals.com**, **canada.creditcards.com**, and **www.rewardscanada.com**. With a few exceptions, credit card issuers in Canada tend to apply competitive—and similar—interest rates, but they apply different rates to purchases, cash advances, and balance transfers. You should compare the rate that you pay with the rates listed at **www.fcac-acfc.gc.ca** just to make sure you're not paying more than you have to.

4. Compare your rate to your credit score

Before you start calling your credit card companies, find out what your credit score is. In Canada, credit bureaus must provide you with a free copy of your credit report, by mail, when you submit a request, by mail. Unfortunately, they don't jump to attention whenever they receive a letter from a consumer asking for a copy of her credit report, because there's nothing in it for them. Fortunately, you can also get a copy of your credit report online at the website of each of the credit reporting companies: TransUnion, Northern Credit Bureaus, or Equifax. Make sure that you ask the company to include a copy of your credit score when it sends you a credit report. The score and the report are not the same thing, and what you want to see is your credit score.

We'll cover everything you need to know about credit scores in the next chapter, but obviously if you have a "super prime" borrower's credit score, then your credit card company should be charging you the lowest available rate. If it isn't, ask why when you call. Remember—unless you make the effort to get your interest rates down by asking for a fair deal or a better deal, your rates will stay high, and it will be harder to get out of debt.

Okay—are you ready? Great. Let's pick up the phone and start what I call the "Credit Card Rate Negotiation Game."

THE CREDIT CARD RATE NEGOTIATION GAME

You are now ready to negotiate. On page 69, you'll find the Debt Free for Life Rate Negotiator Worksheet. Use it to track your efforts—and your progress.

Negotiating your credit card interest rate can be as easy as simply calling your credit card company and asking, "What's my interest rate on this card—and can I get a better one?" Although I've mentioned that this is not always the case, it sometimes is just that simple. A reader of mine named Charlotte recently wrote to me and shared the following story.

> David, I can't believe that lowering my rate on my credit cards was as easy as just asking. I saw you on Oprah discussing this and I did exactly as you said. I carry balances on five credit cards that charge me an average rate of over 20%. Well, I called all five companies, and three of them immediately cut my rate in half! One card offered me zero percent interest for six months if I transferred some new money to them from another card (which I did), and one card refused. Four out of five isn't bad!

The *Wall Street Journal* reported a few years ago that despite all the attention that had been focused on the importance of getting your credit card interest rates reduced, more than 75% of all cardholders hadn't even tried. On the other hand, most of the 25% who did were successful on the first call. Of course, as I said earlier, credit is much tighter today than it used to be and many credit card companies simply will not give you a lower rate. Even worse, instead of lowering your rates when you ask, some companies will respond by raising them. I share this not to scare you out of trying but to make sure you have all the facts.

As a practical matter, credit card interest rates rarely go beyond 29.99%. So if you're currently paying 25% or more, you really have nothing to lose by asking for a lower rate.

DEBT FREE FOR LIFE SUCCESS STORY

This past weekend my husband I read *Start Late, Finish Rich*. We are in our fifties so we definitely feel like we are starting late. We had heard about calling to lower our interest rates on our credit cards—but like everyone else, we asked "really?" Well, yesterday, I used your plan and your scripts—and guess what?! It worked! I called my credit card company and asked them about lowering my rate. We'd been paying an outrageous 24.98% forever. The first person I spoke with said she could lower it to 13.9%. I thought to myself, wow—on the first try. Then I thought, why not be courageous and ask for a rate lower than 10%? I asked to be transferred to a supervisor and the next guy asked me some additional questions—and then he said we can lower your rate to 8.96%, starting next month. Amazing—in just five minutes with one call, the rate went down 16%! I was also able to take another card that was charging me a $120 annual fee and 19.5% interest—and with one call switch that to a new card with a $29 annual fee and only 11.5% interest. I am so excited to Finish Rich—even if we are starting late. Thank you!

Bev J.
New York, NY

WHAT IF I ASK FOR A LOWER RATE AND THEY SAY NO?

When you call the credit card company, your job is to USE YOUR KNOWLEDGE. Remember, you have become smarter about your debt and you now know what kind of rates are being offered, so there's no reason for you to be afraid to ask for a better deal.

When you call a credit card company, you should assume that the first person you speak to is going to say, "Sorry, I can't help you."

This is what the first tier of customer service reps who take calls are generally trained to say.

If this happens, simply respond by saying, "Well, then let me speak to someone who *can* help me. If you can't work with me on getting a better rate, then please connect me with your supervisor."

When you make this request, the customer service rep may say, "I'm sorry—no one is available right now." Don't accept this. Again, it's what they are trained to say. Instead, tell them you want their name and ID number, so you have a record of the person to whom you spoke. Then insist they put a supervisor on the line *immediately*.

Since I first began taking this approach, I have *never* been unable to get a supervisor on the phone. Once you've got him or her on the line, your job is explain your situation. Start by going over your rate, tell them your credit score, and ask why your rate is higher than it should be. Compare your rate to what competitors are offering and ask if they would be willing to work with you to give you a better deal.

HERE'S WHAT HAPPENED WITH MY FRIEND ALICE

After researching her card and her credit score, we knew exactly where she stood. Her credit score was a healthy 740. (We'll discuss credit scores in more detail in the next chapter.) This score qualified her for a "Prime" rate—which at the time was averaging around 15%.

So we called her credit card company. Sure enough, the first person we spoke to said, "Sorry, but there is nothing we can do.

We have raised rates across the board. The rate for all our customers with old cards is now 29%."

At that point, we asked to speak with a supervisor. We were immediately transferred to a new representative, a supervisor named Michael. He looked up Alice's payment record and credit history—and immediately offered to lower her 29% rate to 25%. Now, in my opinion, a 4% rate reduction isn't much, especially when the same credit card is being offered to new customers at a fraction of that rate. Looking at this as a challenge, we politely went over the facts again with Michael. He was very friendly and explained that his hands were tied. "Twenty-five percent is truly the best rate we can give you now," he said. Eventually, Alice accepted the 4% reduction, and went back to searching for a new card a lower rate.

Ultimately, Alice wound up taking advantage of an offer she got in the mail—for a card that was offering new customers zero percent interest for six months! She applied and transferred her existing Visa balance to it. True, she had to pay a transfer fee of $300, but for six months there wouldn't be any additional charges on her debt. Because she read the fine print on her transfer agreement (something you should always do), she knew that if she were just one day late on even one payment, the rate on her new card would be increased retroactively to 25%. So she made a point not to be late—ever!

SOMETIMES IT'S EASIER
TO LOWER YOUR RATE

In Alice's case, before we gave up on her bank, we asked Michael if we could speak with *his* supervisor, and he transferred us to the floor manager. He too said he was unable to do anything for Alice. But this isn't always the case. Sometimes, the second or third supervisor has more authority and can lower the rate even when his subordinates say it's impossible. I know this sounds ridiculous, but it is truly a game!

The reality is that there is almost always something they can do. What you need to know is that credit card companies lower rates all the time, every day of the year, every hour of the day! On the *Oprah* "Debt Diet" show, I worked with one couple who had twelve credit cards, and we were able to ultimately get all but one of them to lower their rates to below 5%. In some cases it took multiple calls, but the effort paid off in the end.

DEBT FREE FOR LIFE SUCCESS STORY

David, I saw you on television talking about how you can pay down your debts faster when you negotiate with the credit card companies and get your rate lowered. Truthfully, I doubted it would work—but I also figured, what do I have to lose? I had seven credit cards—and I followed your advice exactly as you shared it. Four of the seven credit card companies lowered my interest rate on the first call! One credit card company lowered my rate from 24% to 14%! Another credit card was at 14% and it was lowered to below 10%. Three credit card companies refused, and one even raised my rate. So I took your advice and shopped for a new credit card. In the end, I moved my balances to a card that was offering new customers zero percent interest for six months. I figured out that these calls will save me over $1,000 in interest payments in just the first year! Who knew that a few phone calls could put back so much money in my pocket? Thank you so much for your invaluable advice and for your motivation! And I'm not giving up on the two card companies that said "no"—I plan to call them back in 90 days, as you suggested.

Veronica M.
New York, NY

ASK THE CREDIT CARD COMPANIES ABOUT THEIR FORBEARANCE OR DEBT MANAGEMENT PLANS

When all else fails, there is one last resort that can ultimately get your rates lowered. It's a service that the credit card companies don't actively promote and is aimed at what they categorize as "hardship" cases.

The credit card companies know that a proportion of their customers are in financial distress. It may be because you lost a job, had an illness in your family, or are simply earning less than you used to earn (what they call being "underemployed"). What the credit card companies may do in such cases is review your situation. Based on what they find, they may decide to work with you to restructure your debt. This restructuring can include lowering your interest rates to zero for a period of time (usually six months to a year), lowering your minimum payments, suspending over-the-limit penalties or annual fees—or all of the above.

There are two basic types of hardship plans for people with credit card problems, what are known as "Forbearance Plans" and what are called "Debt Management Plans (or DMP Plans)." I have coached people with interest rates on their credit cards as high as 29% who were able to get their rates cut to zero as a result of signing up for one of these plans. As I write this in the summer of 2010, the average rates for these plans range from 0% to 9%.

HOW FORBEARANCE PLANS WORK

Millions of credit card customers have taken advantage of these plans. So trust me—if you apply and are accepted, you will not be alone.*

*www.citibank.com/citi/press2010/100315a_en.pdf

In most cases, the first thing you will have to do is explain your "hardship" so the bank can decide whether or not you qualify for the program. If you qualify, the bank will work out a new payment plan for you. You will then be asked to sign an agreement that commits you to the plan. Read the paperwork closely! The minimum monthly payment will be debited from your chequing account, and your credit account will be frozen. This means you can't use it anymore—which is probably a good thing if you are in debt to the point you need one of these plans.

One downside of enrolling in a forbearance program is that your credit card company may report this fact to the credit bureaus—and if it does, your credit score could go down. But not all the card companies report borrowers who enroll in forbearance programs. To find out whether yours does or not, make sure you read the fine print before you sign the contract.

The truth is that even if enrolling in a forbearance program affects your credit score in the short term, it's better than falling behind on your payments or not being able to reduce your debt because you're paying so much in interest. And if you can't afford to pay off your cards, you will be hurting your credit score anyway.

HOW DEBT MANAGEMENT PLANS WORK

With the assistance of a credit counsellor, you can also work with credit card companies to create a Debt Management Plan, or DMP. We'll cover these more fully in Chapter Eleven, but for now what you need to know is that the primary difference between a forbearance plan and a DMP is the amount of time you have to be in the plan, how much time you have to pay down your debt, and the way you make your monthly payments, usually through a non-profit credit counselling agency. As a rule, the credit card company will discuss your situation with you and your counsellor and then decide if you are a good candidate for a DMP. If you are judged suitable, the credit card company may lower your interest rates and waive fees as long as you as you make the payments required by the plan. In many cases, credit card companies may recommend a DMP—and suggest you work with a non-profit credit counsellor in order to qualify. I will explain in detail how to work with a non-profit credit counselling organization in Chapter Eleven.

DON'T BE DISCOURAGED IF YOU CAN'T DO IT YOURSELF

If you've managed to get control of your credit card debt by following the steps in this chapter, congratulations! You've come a long way.

But if you haven't managed to do it yourself, don't be discouraged. Not everyone is successful at doing this themselves. Lots of people want a professional to help them through this process. Later on, in Chapters Eleven and Twelve, we'll explore the world of professional credit counsellors, how they work, and how you can find one you can trust. Right now, however, let's focus on one of the most important aspects of your financial life—your all-important credit score and the credit reports it is based on.

DEBT FREE FOR LIFE ACTION STEPS

❏ Give yourself credit for how far you have come in your Debt Free for Life Plan.

❏ Fill out the Debt Free for Life Negotiator Worksheet on page 69.

❏ Find out how much interest you're paying on your credit cards and shop around for a better rate.

❏ If necessary, play the Credit Card Rate Negotiation Game.

❏ If you're really in distress, find out about Forbearance and Debt Management Plans.

CHAPTER SEVEN

YOUR CREDIT REPORT AND SCORE: WHAT IT IS, AND HOW TO FIX IT FAST

Today I want you to check your credit report and your credit score. After you finish reading this chapter, I want you to put this book down and go online and pull your credit reports from both of Canada's credit bureaus. Then I want you to pull your credit score.

By law, you are entitled to a free copy of your credit reports (I will show you how to get them). You have to pay for your credit score, and each of the reporting companies uses a different scoring system. It will cost you about $45 to obtain both scores. But it's worth it. So no excuses. Today is the day you find out exactly what your credit reports say and what your credit score number is.

Credit scores range from 300 to 850, and the average credit score in Canada today is around 650. Yours may be lower or higher. Whichever it is, today is the day I want you to face up to it—and begin to work on improving it (regardless of what it is) and protecting it! This chapter will be your guide to getting all of this done.

WHY YOUR CREDIT REPORTS ARE SO IMPORTANT

People talk about your "credit score" all the time. What they often forget is that what makes up your credit score is based on data from your credit report. As the old programmer's saying goes, garbage in, garbage out. If the information in your report is inaccurate, your score will be, too. And studies have shown that more than the majority of people's credit reports contain errors. If the mistake is serious enough, it can make borrowing more expensive and reduce your options for getting a mortgage or loan. It can even keep you from getting a loan or credit card or, in some cases, a job.

So it's vitally important that you check out your credit reports and get any errors corrected as quickly as possible. Fortunately, it's fairly easy to get a free copy of your report and fairly easy to correct any errors you may find in it. Each bureau now has tools on its website (which you'll find below) to get mistakes corrected online. If you don't want to pay a fee for the electronic service, you can order a hard copy and submit corrections by mail.

HOW TO PULL YOUR CREDIT REPORT—FOR FREE

Under federal regulations, the two big credit bureaus (Equifax and TransUnion) are required to provide every consumer who asks with a free copy of their credit report once a year. You can get yours by going online to **canadian-creditreport.com/free.htm**. This website tells you what you need to do to get your free credit report and includes copies of the forms you need. Fill out the forms, include acceptable identification (a copy of your driver's licence, birth certificate, bill statement, etc.) and mail in a request to the reporting company. (For details about your credit report and how you can check it, go to the website of the Financial Consumer Agency of Canada at **www.fcac-acfc.gc.ca/eng/publications/CreditReportScore/CCreditReportScore-eng.asp#checkreport**).

Each of the two credit bureaus has its own database with its own file of information about you and its own way of scoring. So you need to look at the reports from both to make sure that the information each has about you is correct and at least comes close to matching what the other bureau has.

HOW TO GET THOSE ERRORS CORRECTED

Credit-reporting agencies and the banks that provide them with data will correct inaccurate or incomplete information in your report when you point it out to them, as long as you can prove that it's incorrect. When you contact one of the credit bureaus, it then contacts the financial institution that reported the erroneous information. If the financial institution agrees that it made a mistake, the bureau has 30 days to correct your report (90 days in Alberta). If you have proof that an error was made, you can expedite things by providing the proof to both the bureau and the bank you are complaining about.

It is critical you do this work with both bureaus when you find an error. Fixing an error at Equifax won't correct it at TransUnion. They are separate companies that compete with each other, and they do not share information.

With both credit bureaus, you can use the correction form that comes with your credit report or use the form that appears on their websites and then submit the form by mail. You can also contact TransUnion by phone to report an error. If you feel more comfortable sending a registered letter than relying on an online form, here is a sample letter you can use. (The mailing address of each bureau is listed afterwards.)

[Insert Date]
[Insert Name of Credit Agency]

[Insert Address]

RE: Request to correct errors in credit report #[insert your credit report's file number.]

Dear [insert agency's name]:

In reviewing the credit report you sent me on [insert date], I have noticed the following errors:

1. [Describe the first error—e.g., "You list my date of birth as Jan. 1, 1900"]

This is incorrect. The correct information is: [be very specific here and accompany it with proof if you have it—e.g., "As the enclosed copy of my birth certificate shows, my date of birth is July 25, 1963."].

2. [Describe the second error—e.g., "You list me as having an active charge account with Sears."]

This is incorrect. The correct information is: [be very specific here and accompany it with proof if you have it—e.g., "I closed this account on March 15, 2001. Please note the enclosed copy of the letter I sent Sears instructing them to close the account."].

3. [Describe the third error—e.g., "You list me as having made two late payments on my Scotiabank home mortgage."]

This is incorrect. The correct information is: [be very specific here and accompany it with proof if you have it—e.g., "I have made all my mortgage payments on time. Please note the enclosed copy of my latest mortgage statement as well as a letter from Scotiabank confirming this fact."].

My contact information is: [insert your mailing address and phone number.]

Sincerely yours,

[Insert your name]

The contact information for the credit-reporting agencies is as follows.

Equifax Canada Inc.
Box 190 Jean Talon Station
Montreal, PQ H1S 2Z2
(800) 465-7166
www.equifax.com/home/en_ca
You can download a form to correct an inaccuracy in your report at **www.econsumer.equifax.ca/ca/view/common/dispute_process.jsp**

All provinces except Quebec:
TransUnion Consumer Relations Department
P.O. Box 338, LCD1
Hamilton, ON L8L 7W2
(800) 663-9980
www.transunion.ca
You can download a dispute form at **www.transunion.ca/ca/personal/creditdisputes/mail_en.page**

In Quebec:
Centre De Relations Aux Consommateurs TransUnion
1 Place Laval Ouest
Suite 370
Laval, PQ H7N 1A1
(877) 713-3393 or (514) 335-0374 in Montreal.
www.transunion.ca
You can download a dispute form at **www.transunion.ca/ca/personal/creditdisputes/mail_en.page**

YOUR CREDIT SCORE NUMBER
REALLY DOES MATTER

Even in the best of times, your credit score deeply affects your ability to get out of debt and stay out of debt. The worse your credit score, the higher the interest rate you will be charged on money you borrow—if you can get a loan at all. The better your score, the less your debt will cost you—and the quicker you'll be able to pay it off.

I've been talking about the importance of knowing your credit score now for at least a decade. But the truth is that it's never been as important as it is today. As I said earlier, your credit score not only affects your ability to borrow money; it also can affect your ability to get or even keep a job. Employers often check the credit scores of prospective employees. Indeed, I hear every week from people who tell me they think they didn't get a job because of their credit score. People are also losing promotions because of bad credit scores. I recently had the privilege of giving a series of speeches at the Pentagon and the military leaders there told me that they take credit scores so seriously that a bad one can actually prevent a soldier from being promoted. (That's because they consider someone with bad credit to be a security risk.)

JUST LIKE YOUR FINANCES,
YOUR CREDIT SCORE CHANGES ALL THE TIME

Much like your grade average in school, your credit score is a measure of your ability—in this case, your ability to handle credit (otherwise known as your creditworthiness). A good score means you are a safe person to lend money to; a bad one means you may be too risky. Lenders use your score to decide whether they should loan you money and, if so, how much interest they should charge you.

Maybe you were told your credit score when you bought a car or refinanced your house a few years back. Well, don't assume it's still the same today. Your score is based on a variety of factors, all of which reflect some aspect of your financial behaviour—how much you borrow, whether or not you pay your bills on time, etc. The result is a three-digit number that is constantly updated, depending on how and what you're doing financially. With at least half of all Canadians reporting that they spend more than they make, and with 21% of Canadians saying they can no longer handle their debts, there's a good chance that the number of people with a score below 600—meaning lenders will regard them as poor risks— has risen over the last couple of years.

This increase, which is obviously the result of the recession, has raised the percentage of Canadians with bad credit to unprecedented levels. Historically only around 15% of consumers score below 600. Now that number has risen as high as 25%. And since scoring below 600 means that you probably won't able to get credit cards, auto loans, or mortgages under the tighter lending standards banks now use, it's more important than ever to make sure you know what your score is right now.

So even if you pulled your score six months ago, you should pull it again today. And don't worry that pulling your score will affect your rating. Checking on yourself is considered a soft inquiry, which you are allowed to do as much as you want (as opposed to a hard inquiry from a potential lender, too many of which can hurt your score).

IN TRUTH, YOU HAVE MORE
THAN ONE CREDIT SCORE

While everyone says you should check your credit score, what
you should be checking are your *scores*. In fact, you have more
than one. That's because lenders, creditors, and the two national
credit-reporting agencies—Equifax and TransUnion—have
their own particular methods and formulas for calculating
what kind of a credit risk you are. They may also have different
information about you.

Equifax uses a system called the FICO score. Many people
think the term "FICO score" is just another way of saying "credit
score" (sort of the way people call all adhesive bandages Band-
Aids and all facial tissues Kleenex). It's not. While FICO is the
oldest and most popular credit-scoring system, TransUnion
uses its own rating system, which is different than FICO's.

That said, the credit-reporting agencies both base their
individual scoring systems on mathematical models developed by Fair Isaac. So while your FICO score may differ
slightly from the scores calculated by TransUnion, it's not
likely to be wildly different. In other words, if you have a great
FICO score, chances are your credit score from TransUnion
will be pretty good too. The opposite is also true: bad FICO
score, bad score from TransUnion.

YOU'VE GOT YOUR REPORT—
NOW FIND OUT YOUR SCORE

As I mentioned before, your credit report is not your credit
score. Your score is *based* on your reports—and, unfortunately,
while the law gives you free access to your credit report, you

have to pay extra to get the score. The simplest route to get your real credit score is to buy it. You can buy it right now from the two credit bureaus. As of this writing, TransUnion and Equifax both charge about $23 for copies of your credit report and credit score combined.

WHERE TO BUY YOUR CREDIT SCORE

www.equifax.com/home/en_ca
www.creditprofile.transunion.ca

DON'T FALL FOR PHONY CREDIT SCORES

Many websites claim to offer free credit scores (usually called a Credit Report Card or some similar name). More often than not, sites currently offering free credit scores don't really give you your real credit score. Rather, they provide a simulation— and then sell your contact information to online marketers of credit-monitoring services. If you don't want the spam that comes with this, read the small print or the FAQ section of the website before you sign up. Also, if you ever sign up for a free credit score, be sure to read the agreement carefully to see if you will automatically be charged a monthly membership fee after the 30-day trial period. Most websites that offer free credit scores do this. I think having a credit-monitoring service can be worth it, but you should know what you are signing up for before you sign. So read the fine print of any site that says "FREE."

WHAT GOES INTO YOUR CREDIT SCORE—
AND WHAT COMES OUT

So how do the credit-rating companies decide what score to assign you? They take your credit history based on your credit reports and run it through a complicated series of calculations. In the case of FICO, the result is a number somewhere between 300 and 850. This is your FICO score. Anything over 720 is considered good. Score 740 or higher and most lenders will give you their best deals. On the other hand, a score below 600 means you will have trouble getting a loan no matter how high an interest rate you're willing to pay.

On its website, Fair Isaac spells out how it weighs the various factors that go into calculating your score. TransUnion, which uses its own scoring system, considers similar factors, in similar proportions. They are, in order of importance:

- **35% of your score: Payment History.** Do you always pay your bills on time or do you have delinquencies? Any bankruptcies, liens, judgments, garnishments, etc. on your record? PAY ATTENTION TO THIS! Simply paying your bills on time impacts more than a third of your score.

- **30%: Amounts Owed.** How much do you owe? What kinds of debt do you have? What proportion of your total credit limit is being used? Most experts agree that a credit utilization of more than 30% will hurt your score. So if your Visa card has a credit limit of, say, $5,000, you'll want to avoid carrying a balance of more than $1,500 at any one time. According to FICO, more than half of all credit card users manage to do this. On the other hand, one in seven are using more than 80% of their available credit.

- **15%: Length of Credit History**. How long since you opened your first credit account? How old is your oldest active account? (The average is 14 years; the longer your history, the better.) This is why you should not close old accounts you don't use—and why you should still keep credit card accounts open even after you have paid them off.

- **10%: New Credit**. How many accounts have you opened recently? How many recent inquiries by potential lenders have occurred? A lot of new activity makes the credit-rating agencies nervous.

- **10%: Types of Credit Used**. How many different kinds of active credit accounts do you have? A varied mix of credit—e.g., credit cards, instalment loans, mortgages, retail accounts, etc.—is a plus; too much of one type is a minus. According to FICO, the average consumer has 13 active credit accounts at any given time—nine of them for credit cards and four for instalment loans.

FICO and the other companies keep the details of their scoring formulas top-secret. But they are very open about the fact that they are designed to ring alarm bells at the first sign that you're getting in over your head. In 2009, the personal finance columnist Liz Pulliam Weston persuaded FICO to explain exactly how certain actions affect its scoring. The results are worth studying. For example, it turns out that maxing out a credit card can knock anywhere from 10 to 45 points off your credit score—even if you pay off the balance in full right away. Skipping a payment cycle (that is, being more than 30 days late with the minimum payment) can cost you 60 to 110 points. And debt settlements—which happen when you take advantage of one of those programs that promise to "settle your debts for just pennies on the dollar"— will reduce your score by 45 to 125 points. (By the way, getting out of an underwater mortgage by arranging what's called a "short sale"—in which you sell your house for less than you owe and your lender writes off the remaining balance—is generally reported as a settlement.)

Not surprisingly, the real credit-score killers are foreclosure and bankruptcy. Having your mortgage foreclosed will slash your credit score by 85 to 160 points, while declaring bankruptcy can shrink your score by as much as a third, cutting anywhere from 130 to 240 points in one fell swoop. No wonder bankruptcy has been called the nuclear bomb of credit actions.

RAISING YOUR SCORE BY 100 POINTS CAN SAVE YOU $100,000

The average credit score in Canada is around 650. That means that the average Canadian can find lots of room for improvement. It's amazing how dramatically a difference of just 50 to 100 points on your FICO score can change everything when it comes to borrowing money. The following table shows how differing credit scores will affect the mortgage rates banks are willing to offer you.

HOW YOUR CREDIT SCORE AFFECTS YOUR MORTGAGE		
(based on a $300,000, 7-year fixed-rate mortgage)		
Score	Interest Rate	Monthly Payment
760-850	4.650%	$1,547
700-759	4.872%	$1,587
680-699	5.049%	$1,619
660-679	5.263%	$1,659
640-659	5.693%	$1,740
620-639	6.239%	$1,845
Source: Fair Isaac; May 6, 2010		

Among other things, table shows that a person with a credit score of 630 would have to pay $1,845 a month for a $300,000 7-year fixed-rate mortgage, while the monthly payment for someone with a 760 score would be just $1,547. You don't think that's such a big deal? Think again.

Say you're the person with the 630 score. If you could raise it by 130 points—which, as you will see in a minute, you can easily do—you could probably refinance and wind up with a monthly mortgage payment that's roughly $300 less than what you're paying now. Now let's say that instead of spending that extra $300 on something else, you added it to your mortgage payment. (We'll assume that your interest rate remains stable for the life of the mortgage.) In other words, you continued to pay the same monthly amount as before, but now $300 more is going to principal instead of interest. Can you guess what this would do to your ability to pay off your mortgage?

Instead of taking you 30 years to pay it off, you'd be debt free in less than 21 years—and your total interest bill would be reduced by a whopping $126,945.

This is just one example of how improving your credit score can help you get out of debt. So let's get going!

DEBT FREE FOR LIFE SUCCESS STORY

David, I did exactly what you suggested in your book *Start Over, Finish Rich*—and sure enough, in less than a year I have been able to raise my credit score over 60 points. By paying down my debt, always paying on time, and fixing mistakes on my credit report files, my score has gone from 680 to over 740. Thanks to the higher score, I've been able to refinance my home and lock in a 30-year mortgage at 4.25%! I will save over $41,000 in interest because of the refinance. Thank you so much for all you do, and all you share.

Richard S.
Long Island, NY

A 12-STEP ACTION PLAN
TO IMPROVE YOUR SCORE

The simple truth is that raising your score isn't that hard if you know what to do. It's mainly a matter of understanding the factors that the credit bureaus weigh and then figuring out which of them you can change for the better. As I said before, I've coached literally thousands of people on fixing their credit scores, and based on that experience I've developed a 12-step action plan to get your score up quickly and keep it there. I promise you—regardless of where you are starting from, if you follow this plan, in six months your score will be higher than you thought possible.

STEP NO. 1
Get your credit report and check it for errors.

I explained before how common mistakes are in credit reports and how easy it is to get them corrected. Once you get your report from Equifax or TransUnion (preferably, both), go through it with a fine-tooth comb and bring any damaging errors you may find (for example, late payments that were actually paid on time or credit limits that are lower than they should be) to the attention of the credit agency, as I've already discussed. Remember, the credit-reporting agencies will correct inaccurate or incomplete information in your report within 30 days (90 days in Alberta) after they've contacted the financial institution where the mistake originated and confirmed the error. (Occasionally, errors can help you, as when accounts you closed are listed as being open; don't feel obliged to correct these.)

STEP NO. 2
Automate your bill paying so you never miss a deadline.

This may be the most important tip. Missing payments—even just one—can really hurt your credit score. For this reason, I strongly recommend that you that you use your bank's online bill-paying service to automatically transfer a pre-set amount every month from your chequing account to cover at least the minimum payments on all your credit accounts. I personally have every single bill of mine automated in this way. As a result, I never need to worry about being late on any payment, even if I am travelling.

> ### STEP NO. 3
> ### If you have missed payments,
> ### get on it and get current.

It's never too late to clean up your act. Get yourself current as quickly as you can and then stay current. Your score will begin to improve within a few months—and the longer you keep it up, the more noticeable the increase will be. The negative weight FICO gives to bad behaviour, such as delinquencies, lessens over time, so as long as you stay on the straight and narrow, those black marks will eventually disappear from your record for good. But remember—late payments can stay on your record for up to seven years—so get those bills paid on time. The sooner you get a record of paying at least the minimums, the better.

> ### STEP NO. 4
> ### Keep your balance well below your credit limit.

Of all the factors you can control—and improve quickly—how much you owe is probably the most powerful. What makes this especially important is that ever since the credit crunch first hit in the fall of 2008, credit card companies have been cutting customers' credit limits without warning. According to one banking analyst, the amount of credit available to consumers through credit cards and other credit lines has been cut in half in recent years. On a personal basis, this can be devastating to your credit score. Say you've got a $1,000 balance on a card with a $2,000 credit limit—and then the card company slashes your limit to $1,000. Suddenly, you've gone from 50% credit utilization to being maxed out, which can shave 45 points from your credit score. The credit bureaus recommend that you keep your usage below 33% of your available credit. Since there's nothing you can do to protect your score if a credit card company reduces your limit arbitrarily, it's vitally important to keep your credit utilization as low as possible at all times.

STEP NO. 5
Beware of the credit card transfer game.

For years, people have been saving money by transferring high-interest credit card balances to low-interest cards. This can still be helpful, but be aware that using one credit line to pay off another sets off credit-score alarm bells—even if all you're doing is consolidating your accounts. All other things being equal, your credit score will be higher if you have a bunch of small balances on a number of different cards rather than a big balance on just one or two.

STEP NO. 6
If you have rack up high balances,
pay your credit card bill *early*.

The "Amounts Owed" part of your credit score is based on the balance due listed on your most recent credit card statements. So even if you pay your bills in full each month, running up high balances can still hurt your score. You can avoid this problem by paying down all or part of your bill *before* the end of your statement period, thus reducing the balance due that will be reported to the credit bureaus.

> **STEP NO. 7**
> ## Hang onto your old accounts, even if you're not using them.

Part of your credit score is based on how long you have had credit accounts. Closing old accounts shortens your credit history and reduces your total credit—neither of which is good for your credit score. If you have to close an account, close a relatively new one and keep the older ones open. Also, *closing an account will not remove a bad payment record from your report.* Closed accounts are listed right along with active ones.

> **STEP NO. 8**
> ## Use your old cards.

In the aftermath of the credit crunch, the credit card industry has gotten much more strict about closing inactive accounts. This can hurt your credit score, since it reduces the average age of your credit accounts. To prevent this from happening to you, pull out your old cards and start putting at least one charge on each of them every month. This will keep the account open, which in turn will keep your credit history nice and long—and ultimately raise your score.

> **STEP NO. 9**
> ## Demonstrate that you can be responsible.

The best way to raise your score is to demonstrate that you can handle credit responsibly—which means not borrowing too much and paying back what you do borrow on time. Don't open new accounts just to increase your available credit or create a better variety of credit. This is especially true if you are just beginning to establish a credit history. Adding a lot of new accounts may look risky—and it will definitely lower your average age of your accounts, which can hurt your score if you don't have much of a track record. You should open new credit accounts only if and when you need them.

STEP NO. 10

When you're shopping for a loan, do it quickly.

When you apply for a loan, the lender will "run your credit"— that is, send an inquiry to one of the credit-rating agencies to find out how creditworthy you are. Too many such inquiries can hurt your credit score, since they could indicate you're trying to borrow money from many different sources. Of course, you can generate a lot of inquiries doing something perfectly reasonable—like shopping for the best mortgage or auto loan by applying to a number of different lenders. The FICO scoring system is designed to allow for this by considering the length of time over which a series of inquiries are made. Try to do all your loan shopping within 30 days, so the inquires get batched together and it's obvious to FICO that you are loan shopping.

STEP NO. 11

Know the difference between a "soft inquiry" and a "hard inquiry."

Fair Isaac and the credit bureaus all recognize the difference between you checking your own score (what is called a "soft inquiry") and the banks or lending organizations checking your score (a "hard inquiry"). While too many hard inquiries can lower your score, soft inquiries don't count against you at all. So feel free to check your credit score as often as you want.

STEP NO. 12
Consider buying a credit-monitoring package and identity-theft service.

I am constantly urging my readers not to sign up for unnecessary monthly expenses. That said, I really do think that your credit score and your credit report are so important that it makes sense to pay for a credit and identity theft monitoring service. Both of Canada's credit bureaus will sell you such a monitoring service for roughly the same price, around $14.95 a month. I personally pay for this kind of service myself because I think it's worth the investment.

Congratulations! You now know more than 95% of all Canadians about what may well be the most important influence over your financial life—your credit record and score. Now let's look at how to handle what is probably the biggest single debt you will ever have.

DEBT FREE FOR LIFE ACTION STEPS

- ❑ Go to **canadian-creditreport.com/freebymail.htm** and start the process of applying for your credit reports from the two major credit bureaus.
- ❑ Check the reports for errors and, if you find any, request a correction immediately.
- ❑ Apply to the two credit-reporting agencies for your credit score.
- ❑ Follow the 12-step plan to improve your score.

CHAPTER EIGHT

MORTGAGE DEBT:
HOW TO PROTECT YOUR HOME
AND PAY OFF YOUR MORTGAGE EARLY

If you're a homeowner, your mortgage is almost certainly the biggest single debt you have—or ever will have. In fact, your mortgage is probably several times bigger than all your other debts put together. Indeed, as I write this in the summer of 2010, statistics show that Canadians owe a total of $971 billion in home mortgage debt—compared to about $300 billion in auto loans, credit card balances, and every other kind of consumer debt.

So if you're going to be debt free for life, the place to start is figuring out how to pay off your mortgage as quickly as possible. And that's what this chapter is about. In the pages that follow, I'm going to share with you my foolproof plan to pay any mortgage off years early—and save tens of thousands of dollars or more in interest charges.

I'll also show you how to make sure you have the right kind of mortgage, what to do if you don't, and then finally what to do if you are having trouble making your payments. The fact is, for many of us these days, the issue isn't how fast we can pay off our mortgage, but whether we can pay it off at all. The good news is that there are a variety of programs designed to make your mortgage more affordable. By the time we're finished here, you'll know exactly who to call and where to go to get your interest rate lowered and maybe even your principal amount reduced.

PAY OFF YOUR MORTGAGE EARLY— AND SAVE HUNDREDS OF THOUSANDS OF DOLLARS IN THE PROCESS

For homeowners, the key to becoming debt free for life is paying off your mortgage as quickly as possible. Of course you can't even think about doing that unless you have the right kind of mortgage—which is to say, a long-term fixed mortgage with payments you can afford to make. Later on in this chapter, I'll explain what you should do if you don't have the right mortgage. But for the moment, let's assume you do. How do you pay it off as quickly as possible?

Well, if you can manage the higher monthly payments, there is no question that signing up for a 15-year fixed amortization is the way to go. Not only will you be free of your mortgage debt sooner, but also you will save a lot of money in the process. And when I say a lot, I mean A LOT.

Let's say you have a $200,000 mortgage with a 6% interest rate. As the table below shows, paying it off in 15 years instead of 25 would reduce the total cost of the loan by more than a third—a savings to you of roughly *$82,000!* Of course, your monthly payments would be $400.16 higher with the shorter term ($1,679.77 a month vs. $1,279.61 a month), but if you can manage to write the bigger cheque, it will pay off for you big time over the long run. Just think what you could do with an extra $82,000. This is definitely a case where a little short-term pain equals a huge long-term gain.

Many of you are worried about the stock market, and whether or not you can trust it. The one investment you can definitely trust today is debt reduction—which is why paying down your mortgage is such a smart investment in an uncertain world.

COST OF A 15-YEAR AND A 25-YEAR FIXED MORTGAGE Amount: $300,000 Annual Interest: 6.00%		
	15-year mortgage	25-year mortgage
Monthly payment	$1,679.77	$1,279.61
Total interest	$102,357.81	$183,883.97
Total payments	$302,357.81	$383,883.97
SOURCE: ATB.com		

WHAT IF A 15-YEAR MORTGAGE IS JUST TOO EXPENSIVE FOR YOU?

I know that, especially these days, most people simply can't afford to make the higher monthly payments that go along with a 15-year fixed mortgage. But that doesn't mean there's nothing you can do to speed up the day when your home will be debt free.

In my previous books, I've described a simple system that any homeowner can use to pay off a 25-year mortgage as much as seven years early. When people hear about it, they often think it's a trick.

Well, it's not.

Think about it this way. The problem with a 25-year mortgage is that it's designed to make you spend 25 years paying it off! Let's stick with our example of a $200,000 mortgage at 6%. If you take the full 25 years to pay it off, you will wind up actually giving the bank close to $385,000, since in addition to paying back the principal, you will also make nearly $185,000 in interest charges.

Here's a better approach. What if you were to take that same mortgage and make the payments on a biweekly instead of a monthly schedule? I know it's hard to believe, but this simple change can cut the total payment time by six years—and in the process save you almost $35,000 in interest charges.

PAY YOUR MORTGAGE FASTER— PAINLESSLY

Here's how it works. All you do is take the normal 25-year mortgage you have and instead of making the monthly payment the way you normally do, you split it down the middle and pay half every two weeks.

Say your mortgage payment is $1,279.61 a month (which is what it is in the example we used above). Under my biweekly plan, instead of sending a cheque for that amount to your mortgage lender (or having it withdrawn automatically from your account) once every month, you would pay $639.81 every two weeks. At the beginning, paying $639.81 every two weeks probably won't feel any different than paying $1,279.61 once a month. But as anyone who's ever looked at a calendar could tell you, it's not really the same thing. A month, after all, is a little longer than four weeks. And so what happens as a result of switching to a biweekly payment plan is that over the course of a year you gradually get further and further ahead in your payments, until by the end of the year you have paid the equivalent of not 12 but 13 monthly payments. Best of all, because it is so gradual, you will hardly feel the pinch.

The math is actually quite simple. A monthly mortgage payment of $1,279.61 amounts to $15,355.32 a year. But when you make a half payment every two weeks instead of a full one once a month, you end up making 26 half payments over the course of a year. That's 26 payments of $639.81—for a total of $16,635.06, or one extra month's worth of payments, painlessly.

DEBT FREE FOR LIFE SUCCESS STORY

Taking your advice on paying down principal early, I have set up my mortgage payments automatically and I submit two full extra payments per year. At this rate, my home will be paid off in twelve years versus thirty and I will have saved tens of thousands of dollars in interest—not mention that the house (now a rental) is bringing in positive cash flow. I will be financially comfortable by age 43, with all the leisure time in the world to enjoy life and pursue other business and investment opportunities. Best of all I will have NO mortgage. Thanks again!

Marc B.
San Diego, CA

WHAT COULD YOU DO WITH AN EXTRA $35,000?

The impact of that extra month's payment is awesome. Depending on your interest rate, you will end up paying off a 25-year mortgage four years early! You will be debt free years ahead of schedule, saving you tens of thousands of dollars in interest charges over the life of your loan.

I'm not just making up these figures. Check out the table below. It shows the difference between a monthly and a biweekly payment plan for a $200,000 25-year mortgage with an interest rate of 6%. The monthly pay-off schedule winds up incurring a total of $183,883.97 in interest charges over the life of the loan. The biweekly schedule, on the other hand, runs up just $148,910.17 in interest. In other words, switching to the biweekly plan will save you almost $35,000.

MONTHLY PAYMENTS VS. BIWEEKLY PAYMENTS				
Principal = $200,000 Interest Rate = 6.00 % Amortization = 25 years				
Payment Frequency	Monthly Payment	Actual Amortization (years)	Total Interest Costs	Interest Saved
Monthly	$1,279.61	25	$183,883.97	N/A
Biweekly	$639.81	21	$148,910.17	$34,973.80

If you'd like to figure out how much you could save on your own mortgage, go online and visit my website at **www.finishrich.com.** First, click on "Learn," then look under "Free Resources" and click the "Get a biweekly mortgage payment plan" Calculator. This will take you to the best free calculator I've found on the Internet. You can then plug in your own numbers and quickly see how much you could save by switching to a biweekly payment plan.

ALL IT TAKES IS FIVE MINUTES

The great thing about switching to a biweekly payment plan is that it allows you to save money over the long run without refinancing or otherwise changing your mortgage. All it takes is one call.

That's because these days most mortgage lenders offer programs designed to totally automate the process I've just described. To enroll, all you need to do is phone your lender or go to its website. If your mortgage is with one of the Big Six banks, you may have to pay a one-time setup fee, but the bank will automate the process for you.

WHY NOT DO IT YOURSELF?

Why spend hundreds of dollars on an outside firm when you could just as easily use your bank's online automatic bill-paying service to schedule biweekly mortgage payments for yourself? Unfortunately, it's not really that simple.

The problem is that if you split your monthly mortgage payment in half and send it in to your mortgage lender every two weeks yourself, the lender will simply send it back to you because staff won't know what to do with it. Or worse, they'll stick the money in an escrow account and just let it sit there. Believe it or not, standard operating procedure at many banks is to take extra payments and hold them in a non-interest-bearing account—not use them to pay down your mortgage.

WHAT YOU COULD DO FOR FREE

You could add 10% to your regular mortgage payment each month and have the money applied toward the principal. Or you could make one extra payment at the end of the year and again have it go towards your principal. But note that word "could." Let's face it—some things are much easier said than done.

If you decide to do it yourself, my suggestion is that you add an extra 10% a month towards your mortgage payment—*and make the payment automatic.* (To learn how to make it automatic, see Chapter Fourteen.) Also, make a point of asking your bank to make sure that this extra payment is credited towards your principal—and then check your monthly statements to make sure the bank did it correctly.

PENNY-WISE OR POUND-FOOLISH?

Some people are put off by the cost of a biweekly payment. But think about it. When all is said and done, running a biweekly payment plan shouldn't cost you more than $100 a year. For this modest expense (less than $2,500 over the life of the loan), you will save tens of thousands of dollars. In the example I provided earlier, the savings totalled almost $35,000. Some readers have told me this one idea saved them more than twice that!

And a biweekly payment plan does more than allow you to pay off your home early. It also makes it easier to manage your money, since most of us get paid every two weeks. You'll be richer faster, with a plan that makes your life easier. As I say, it's a key part of being debt free for life.

FROM BOOM TO BUST: THE HOMEOWNER'S NIGHTMARE

As I write this in the summer of 2010, Canada has gone through a period of falling real estate values and tight lending. Canada didn't suffer the way some communities did in the United States, where house prices dropped by an average of about 30%. But the turbulence was enough to put some Canadian homeowners in a tight spot. The number of homeowners in arrears has risen to a seven-year high, according to the Canadian

Bankers Association. That means they've gone three straight months without making a payment. (To put this into perspective, however, I should add that only 17,000 mortgages are in arrears out of a total of 4.1 million, so it's not an epidemic by any means.) Still, Canadians are deeper in debt than ever. The average household in Canada owes 145% more in mortgage and consumer loan debt than it earns in income. House prices on average are five times as high as the after-tax income of Canadian households, and most people under the age of thirty-four say they'd be in trouble if their paycheque was delayed by even a week. In other words, people's pockets aren't bulging with cash to buy a house.

Those who have read my other books know that I've always been a great advocate of homeownership. Nothing you will ever do in your lifetime is likely to make you as much money as buying a home and living in it. Despite the pain and turmoil of the last few years, I still believe this. As I see it, the most important real estate lesson we can draw from what we've been through is simply that there are no shortcuts to successful homeownership. There are two rules in particular that you should always follow: (1) always make sure you have the right kind of mortgage; and (2) never borrow more than you can afford to pay back. In other words, never buy a home that you can't comfortably afford.

WHAT DO YOU DO IF YOU DON'T HAVE THE RIGHT KIND OF MORTGAGE?

As I said at the beginning of this chapter, my early pay-off plan won't work unless you have the right kind of mortgage— a fixed-rate mortgage with a twenty-five-year amortization and payments you can afford. There are few surprises with such a mortgage: you know exactly what your payments will be for the term of the mortgage and you pay down principal with every payment, reducing the amount you owe and building equity every month. Most mortgage lenders in Canada offer fixed-rate mortgages for as long as ten years.

So my recommendation is that if you plan to be in your home more than another five years and you have anything but a fixed-rate mortgage, then you should refinance NOW. Rates are at historic lows as I write this—but this won't last forever.

The best place to start mortgage shopping is online. First, go to a website like **www.canequity.com/rates/** or **www.bankrate. com** (click on the Canadian flag at the bottom of the page) and see what mortgage lenders are offering. Then call your current lender and ask if he can match the best deal you found online.

WHAT YOU NEED TO KNOW ABOUT REFINANCING

Lending standards are much tighter than they used to be, but if you can meet the requirements, most banks will be happy to refinance your mortgage. The three basic criteria are:

- **Your debt-to-income ratio, or DTI.** Mortgage lenders want your DTI to be less than 30%. That is, your monthly mortgage payments, including principal and interest, plus property taxes, shouldn't total more than 30% of your monthly income.

- **Your loan-to-value ratio, or LTV.** Most lenders want it to be less than 75%—meaning the total amount you owe on your house should be no more than 75% of what the house is worth. (For example, if your house is worth $200,000, they will not refinance a mortgage of more than $150,000.)

- **Your credit score.** As I noted in Chapter Seven, you'll generally need a FICO score of at least 620 to even be considered for a loan—and at least 740 to get the best interest rates.

When you compare mortgages, you will need to make note of the interest rate and whether the lender will require an appraisal, title search, title insurance, credit reports, etc., which can drive up the closing costs.

Refinancing makes sense only if the savings you enjoy from lower interest charges more than cover the cost of closing the new mortgage. If you will be in your home for more than another three years, you'll generally come out ahead as long as your new interest rate is at least one full percentage point lower than what you are currently paying. Have your bank run a "break-even analysis" for you. They can do this in a matter of minutes and tell you, "Yup, the cost of refinancing will be paid off in 28 months [or whatever]." You need to know this before you pull the trigger on your "refi."

WHAT DO YOU DO IF YOU CAN'T AFFORD TO MAKE YOUR MORTGAGE PAYMENTS?

The worry of losing your home can be paralyzing—but when you are faced with foreclosure, doing nothing is the biggest mistake you can make.

Compared to the United States, where lenders provided mortgages to anyone who could breathe, Canadian mortgage lenders have stuck to the rules, providing mortgages only to people who can afford to pay them back. As a result, relatively few people in this country find themselves in the position of being faced with foreclosure.

That doesn't mean that Canadians will never find themselves in trouble. Unemployment, illness, family crises, and legal problems can all create situations that put pressure on people who have to pay a mortgage.

If you're having trouble making a mortgage payment, take action immediately. The worst thing you can do is stall for time or try to sweep the problem under the carpet.

Here's what you should do:

1. **Call your lender immediately.** The single biggest mistake borrowers make when they fall behind on their mortgage is not contacting their lender. As soon as you realize you have a problem, you've got to make that call. The foreclosure process for most lenders has a set schedule, so the longer you wait the fewer options you'll have.

2. **Ask to speak to the loss mitigation department.** See if your monthly statement contains the phone number to the lender's loss mitigation department. If not, call the customer service number and ask for that department. At most lenders, the loss mitigation department helps borrowers determine which workout option they qualify for. Keep in mind, though, that some lenders have their collections departments advise borrowers on workout options, so don't be alarmed if you're sent straight to collections.

3. **Be prepared to review your situation in detail with your lender.** Your lender will ask a series of questions to assess your financial situation. Some lenders have specialists with

both the training and technology to pre-qualify a caller for a workout option right over the phone. If you have the right financial documents in front of you when you make the call, you might be able to get a resolution within minutes. So organize your bills, statements, and anything else that will help give an accurate picture of your current financial status. And resist the temptation to make your financial situation sound better than it really is. All that will accomplish is to get you a workout agreement that won't really help you. (By the same token, don't exaggerate how bad your situation is. That may lead your lender to think there's no way you can keep your house.)

4. **Know the ways your lender can help you avoid foreclosure.** According to Consolidated Credit Counselling Services of Canada Ltd. (**www.consolidatedcredit.ca**), most people take out a second mortgage when they get behind in their mortgage payments. Depending on how serious your situation is, your lender can offer you other retention options (ways to keep your house) or liquidation options (ways to give up your house without going into foreclosure). Other retention options include forbearance (which generally lets you pay less than the full amount of your mortgage payment for a temporary period), a repayment plan (where you pay off your overdue mortgage payments in instalments), reinstatement (where you agree to pay your lender everything you owe in one lump sum by a specific date) and loan modification (where your interest rate and other loan conditions are changed). Liquidation options include a short sale (where your lender agrees to accept an offer to buy your house for less than the amount you owe, which then cancels the debt), deed in lieu of foreclosure (where you voluntarily

transfer your property to your lender), and assumption (which allows a qualified buyer to take over your mortgage and make the payments). If you have a CMHC-insured loan, you may have additional options available to you. It's important to check with your lender for details.

5. **Know where to turn if you aren't getting the help you need from your lender.** There are a number of non-profit credit counselling organizations that will help you if you get into trouble with paying your mortgage. Consolidated Credit Counselling Services of Canada is one. Another is Credit Counselling Canada (**www.creditcounsellingcanada.ca**).

REMEMBER, YOU HAVE TO LIVE SOMEWHERE

My last words of advice regarding your home and your mortgage is to keep in mind that you have to live somewhere. The beauty of owning your own home is that if you pay down your mortgage, the cost of homeownership will eventually be cheaper than renting. One of the biggest mistakes homeowners make when house prices rise is to treat their homes like they were ATM machines, continually drawing on their home equity lines of credit to pay for consumer goods—and to pay off credit card debt.

It's time now to go back to the basics of home ownership, where you buy less than you can afford and pay off your home faster. Real estate markets in Canada are relatively stable, especially compared to the United States. Ultimately we will see home prices begin to appreciate again. But for you, right now and forever, the key is to focus on paying down your debt.

A debt-free home is a really nice home to live in—and it's absolutely worth striving for!

DEBT FREE FOR LIFE ACTION STEPS

❑ Use the mortgage calculators at **www.finishrich.com** to see how much more quickly you could pay off your mortgage—and how much you could save—by switching to a biweekly payment plan.

❑ If you don't have a fixed-rate mortgage with payments you can afford, ask your lender for a better deal and start shopping around online.

❑ If you can't afford your mortgage and are unable to re-finance, take action immediately.

CHAPTER NINE

THE STUDENT LOAN DIET: NINE GREAT WAYS TO CRUSH YOUR STUDENT DEBT AND SLEEP WELL AT NIGHT

This chapter is for anyone who has taken out student loans to pay for their education. It's also for anyone who may be considering borrowing money for post-secondary studies in the future.

Over the last two years, I have received more questions about student loans than I got in the previous two decades combined. The reason is brutally simple: Universities and community colleges are more expensive than ever (which makes borrowing harder to avoid). And, because of the recession, it's also the hardest time in decades for graduates to find decent employment—and thus earn the money they need to be able to pay off their loans.

This financial double-whammy is crushing a generation of young people under a mountain of debt many find impossible to manage. The majority of Canadian young people acquire some form of higher education by the time they're 24. This places Canada at the top of all countries in the Organisation for Economic Co-operation and Development (OECD) in educational attainment. But it comes at a price.

Six in 10 university students and 45% of community college students borrow money under Canada's student loan program by the time they graduate. According to the Canadian Council on Learning, the average university student owes almost $27,000 upon graduation. As of September 2010, the federal student loan program had reached its maximum lending level of $15 billion, prompting the federal government to add another $2 billion to the pot for the 50,000 post-secondary students heading to community colleges and universities across the country.

Yet according to Statistics Canada, as many as four in five students fail to start repaying their loans upon graduation. That puts them into delinquency, and delinquency when it comes to repaying your debts can have serious consequences.

A lot of people are borrowing a lot of money to pay for an important step in their lives. Some become so burdened by debt that they drop out of school before they complete their program. So let's look at how you should borrow money for school—and ultimately get it paid off!

TIP NO. 1:
Get the facts and understand the problem.

A generation ago, student loans seemed reasonable and easily managed. Now they're a nightmare!

Driven by post-secondary costs that are increasing rapidly, borrowing for education has exploded. A full-time post-secondary education in Canada now costs almost $15,000 a year, including books, housing, transportation, and other expenses. Tuition alone costs as much as $8,000 a year, and it's rising faster than the rate of inflation. Between 2009 and 2010, for example, tuition for an undergraduate education increased by more than 5% in Ontario and by 4% in Canada as a whole. No wonder student debt has more than doubled in the last 20 years.

In the past I have argued that student loans are not only a good investment (because higher education generally leads to increased earnings potential) but also that they are a more intelligent form of debt than, say, a bank loan you might take out to buy a boat or car or a credit card balance you run up to pay for a vacation. In recent years, however, I have begun to see some problems with student loans.

To begin with, people who borrow money for their post-secondary education often don't really understand what a serious commitment they're making. It's generally easier to get a student loan than it is to borrow money to buy a home or a car or get a credit card—and yet student loans are just as difficult as conventional loans to get out of if you get into financial trouble.

More disturbing, though, is that increasing debt forces students to undervalue their higher education. For the fact remains, in Canada, at least, that a post-secondary certificate or degree enables you to make more money or at least remain employed when others lose their jobs. According to a 2009 study based on data compiled by the Canadian Millennium Scholarship Foundation, working Canadians with a bachelors degree earned almost $20,000 a year more than individuals with a high school education. In the meantime, unemployment rates among young men without a high school education rose by 7% between 1971 and 2005. Among young men with a university degree, the rate rose by only 1% over the same period.

The trouble is, none of this seems to matter when you borrow money for school. You may be betting that you'll be able to afford to pay back the loan after you graduate, and you probably will. But it may take longer than you think; you may feel anxious, worried and pressured in the meantime, and you may have to make sacrifices along the way to repay the money.

Most students seem prepared for this. According to a survey conducted by BMO Financial Group, 28% of students aged eighteen to twenty-four believe they'll struggle to pay off the cost of their education, and 32% think they'll be in debt for years to come. But all of them must wonder occasionally if they made the right decision when they enrolled in community college or university instead of getting a job.

It's because of these factors that this chapter is so important to your Debt Free for Life Plan.

TIP NO. 2:
Student loans affect your life after graduation.

It's important to understand that, if you borrow money for your post-secondary education, you're expected to pay it back. If you fall behind on your payments and don't take steps to relieve yourself of your obligation, your employment income can be garnished, your credit score will suffer, and you can be rendered ineligible for some government jobs. Even by declaring bankruptcy, you can't relieve yourself of the obligation to repay a student loan.

The good news is that student loan programs in Canada are designed to accommodate different individuals who follow different paths after graduation. The typical student loan in Canada is amortized over 10 years. That means that monthly payments are geared to a 10-year repayment period, or 240 months. But according to data collected by the Canadian Millennium Scholarship Foundation, some individuals repay their loans much sooner than that, while others extend the terms of their loans by several years. One in seven graduates, for example, repays his or her student loan in full within two years of graduation, while about half of all graduates take more than two years to repay their loans.

Most people are in their early to mid-twenties when they graduate from community college or university. That means there's a good chance that you'll be repaying your student loan at the same time as you're going through other major events in your life, like marriage, buying a home, and having children.

> **TIP NO. 3:**
> **Understand your repayment options.**

Before you start repaying a student loan, you should understand your options. You can begin by making some calculations using the loan repayment estimator provided at the federal government's CanLearn website (tools.canlearn.ca).

As you'll see, you can make several choices that have a major impact on your monthly payment, the amount of interest you pay and the total amount that you pay over the period of repayment.

For example, let's say you have a student loan equivalent to the average in Canada, $27,000. In selecting the way that you repay the loan, you can choose a fixed or floating interest rate. With a fixed rate, you pay the prime rate of interest plus 5%. With a floating rate, you pay prime plus 2.5%. Even though a floating rate may look more attractive, a fixed rate makes your repayments predictable and gives you some certainty. Floating rates can change from one month to the next, and the rate may go higher than the fixed rate plus 5%.

You can choose to take advantage of a six-month grace period, during which you'll be charged interest even though you don't have to make any payments. You can also choose the number of months you want to take to pay back the loan, to a maximum of 180 months.

I recommend choosing a fixed interest rate. With a fixed rate, you know exactly how much you have to pay every month and how much of your payment goes toward interest costs and how much goes toward paying down the principal.

If you choose to start repayments immediately, without taking the six-month grace period, and you decide to repay the loan in five years at a fixed rate of 2.75%, you'll pay $544.24 per month, and you'll pay a total of $32,654.27. That means your total interest cost on the loan will be $5,654.27.

Alternatively, let's say you choose to take the six-month grace period and incorporate the interest that accumulates over that six months into your loan balance. And you decide to take the entire 174 months (180 – 6-month grace period) to pay back your loan. Now you'll pay just $268.84 a month. But after 180 months you'll have repaid the loan itself plus $18, 731.15 in interest.

Bigger monthly payments, less interest, and shorter time to pay off the loan. Smaller payments, more interest, and longer pay-off time. It's your choice. But I suggest that you choose the shortest term that you can afford.

TIP NO. 4:
What happens if you can't pay?

If you have trouble repaying your student loan, you may be eligible for Repayment Assistance. But as with a conventional loan, mortgage, or other form of debt, you have to let the lender know about your difficulties before you can do anything about them. Sweeping the problem under the rug doesn't work.

The Repayment Assistance Plan operates in two stages. If you qualify, over the first five years of your loan you make affordable payments toward the principal of your loan. This reduces your total debt, while the government covers the interest costs. Your payments will not exceed 20% of your income.

After five years, if you're still in financial difficulty, the government will continue to cover the interest on your loan and start repaying a portion of the principal, as well, while you continue to make payments that you can afford.

In general, you will also not have to repay your loan over a period that's longer than 15 years.

In Ontario, Saskatchewan, Newfoundland and Labrador, and New Brunswick, the provincial and federal student loan programs are integrated. In other provinces, you'll have to notify both programs to see if you're eligible for repayment assistance.

You can contact the National Student Loans Service Centre at 1-888-815-4514 and find more information about repayment assistance at **www.canlearn.ca**.

You can also find information about each of the provincial and territorial student loan programs and their repayment assistance options at **www.canlearn.ca**.

> **TIP NO. 5:**
> **What happens if you want to pay more or less?**

As I indicated above, extending the repayment term on your student loans will cost you thousands of dollars in extra interest charges and delay the day when you finally become debt free. For this reason, I urge you to stick with the ten-year repayment plan unless you truly can't afford it.

Canada's student loan programs allow you to revise the terms of your loan. Not only can you arrange to pay less but also if you find yourself in financial difficulty, you can arrange to pay more if you want to repay your debt more quickly.

For example, you might have landed a good job after graduation and anticipated that you could pay off your loan in five years. But after three years, your job disappears or you have to move to another company at a lower salary.

You can apply through the National Student Loans Service Centre for a Revision of Terms. Your revised loan agreement may allow you to temporarily extend the term of your loan, so that you pay less per month. Or you may choose to make a permanent revision, lowering your payments for the entire term of the loan.

Alternatively, you may choose to increase the monthly payment, either temporarily or permanently. This will allow you to repay your loan more quickly.

You can get more information about reducing or increasing your payments through a Revision of Terms at: **www.canlearn.ca/eng/after/cant/ryp.shtml**.

TIP NO. 6:
Ditch your loans asap.

The bottom line with student loans is this: the fastest way to get rid of them is to live beneath your means and pay them off as quickly as you can. If you've got student loans and you want to have any chance of finishing rich, it is imperative that you move paying them off to the top of your list of financial priorities.

You should want student loans out of your life as quickly as possible because they limit your financial options. As long as you have a loan outstanding, you're tying up several hundred dollars a month in repayments. You could put that money to better use.

As I've said elsewhere in this book, even a small amount of money can make a difference to your financial future if it accumulates over time. And the amount of money that you have to repay every month toward your student loan is not small. It usually adds up to thousands of dollars a year.

Even though the interest rate on your loan is not unreasonable, and even if you've followed my recommendation and chosen a fixed rate of interest, it still makes sense to pay off your student loan as quickly as you can. The sooner you get rid of the debt, the sooner you can start applying the money to something more productive.

TIP NO. 7:

Don't forget to deduct your interest costs when you file your taxes.

Under Canada's *Income Tax Act*, you can claim the interest on your student loan on your income tax return.

I hear from people all the time who have been diligently paying off their student loans for years—only to discover that they had either forgotten or not realized in the first place that they're eligible for the income tax credit on student loan interest.

The financial institution that administers your student loan will send you a summary of your payments every year that includes the total amount of interest that you've paid that year. To receive the income tax credit, you have to indicate this amount on line 319 on your tax return.

As I've already shown you, the interest on a student loan adds up to thousands of dollars. On the average loan of $27,000 you could pay almost $19,000. That's a lot of interest. Since Canada doesn't give you credit for interest on any other type of loan, you should jump at the chance to get credit for your student loan.

TIP NO. 8:

Think before you borrow.

If you haven't yet taken the plunge to borrow money for school but are considering it, then consider this: you need to think through what is a reasonable amount to borrow for an education.

Financial aid expert Mark Kantrowitz, the founder of a U.S. organization called FinAid.org, advises students to limit their borrowing to an amount equal to the annual salary they expect to make their first year out of school. The problem with this approach is that it requires you to predict your income four, five, or six years down the road—and not only be right about the economic outlook, but also about the kind of job (if any) you're going to wind up having.

A better approach would be to keep your borrowing to the absolute minimum. Let's say you pursue a four-year under-graduate degree. According to the Canada Student Loan website, CanLearn.ca, you'll need almost $60,000 to cover the cost of tuition, books, housing, and other expenses. Some of those expenses you'll cover yourself with your income from summer jobs and perhaps from part-time work. Your parents may also contribute. Combining these resources with your student loans, you should be able to afford a post-secondary education without borrowing much more than the average of $27,000. That's not exactly a lifetime sentence of indentured servitude. In fact, if you remain on track after you obtain your degree, your status as a university graduate should enable you to land a well-paying job that will allow you to repay your loan within 10 years.

Keep in mind that there's a limit to the amount of time you can receive student loans to help you cover the cost of your post-secondary education. Full-time students in undergradu-ate and masters programs can receive assistance for a maximum of 340 weeks. Doctoral students are eligible for 400 weeks. Once you reach the limit, interest starts to accumulate on your loans, although you don't have to start repayment until you finish your program or leave school.

TIP NO. 9:
A degree chan change your life—but so can debt.

Getting a degree is one of the most powerful things you can do to improve your life: it broadens your horizons, gives you career flexibility, sets you up to earn more money, and provides numerous other psychic benefits. But if you finance post-secondary education by borrowing too much—or if you mismanage the debt you have incurred—the benefits of a higher education can be quickly outstripped by its costs.

I'm personally in favour of getting the best education you can afford—but the key word is "afford"! Sometimes we borrow more than is really necessary for a post-secondary education. If you have to borrow money to attend the school of your choice, consider whether or not the additional cost is worth the extra burden of debt you will take on. Remember, it's a debt you will probably be paying off for at least a decade.

DEBT FREE FOR LIFE ACTION STEPS

- ❏ Make sure you know what kind of student loans you have and what their repayment options are.
- ❏ If you are having trouble paying off your student loans, check out your repayment assistance options.
- ❏ Make it a priority to pay off any student loans you may have.

CHAPTER TEN

ERASE YOUR DEBT
WITH THREE SIMPLE WORDS:
"TIME-BARRED DEBT"

What would you say if I told you there was a totally legal way to get rid of some or all of your debt IMMEDIATELY—without having to declare bankruptcy, ruin your credit score, or pay big fees to a lawyer?

I know. By now, you've learned that if something sounds too good to be true, it probably is. But there are a few exceptions to that common-sense rule—and this is one of them.

Now before I share this incredible information, please know that I am not a lawyer—and I am not giving legal advice here. Neither am I suggesting that anyone borrow money and not pay it back. But I am your advocate—and you deserve to know the truth about your legal rights so you can make the appropriate decisions for yourself. Just remember this: before you do anything based on the information in this chapter, please consult a lawyer! This chapter is filled with web addresses to visit and telephone numbers to call to get help.

SIMPLE FAIRNESS SAYS YOU SHOULD
BE ABLE TO GET ON WITH YOUR LIFE

You're probably familiar with the idea of a statute of limitations. A statute of limitations is a law that sets a limit on how much time you have after an offence has been committed to take legal action against someone. In criminal offences, it's more common in the United States than Canada. Many states impose a statute of limitations on crimes such as grand theft. If the authorities haven't laid a charge after six years, they can no longer prosecute. In Canada, there's no statute of limitations on such crimes. Authorities can lay charges after one year or twenty. The only exception is treason, which carries a limitation of three years.

The same goes for civil actions. Depending on the province, you have a minimum of one year and a maximum of six years to launch a civil action for damages arising from personal injury, medical malpractice, and other civil matters.

There are good reasons for a statute of limitations. For one thing, the longer a case drags on, the more likely it is that evidence will be lost or damaged, that memories will fade, and that the truth will be harder to determine. But perhaps even more important, our basic sense of fairness includes the notion that, after a reasonable amount of time, potential defendants should either be charged or allowed to get on with their lives. People shouldn't have to live indefinitely with the possibility that they might one day be hauled into court.

JUST BECAUSE YOU STILL OWE IT, DOESN'T MEAN THEY CAN COLLECT IT

So what does all this have to do with getting out of debt? Well, believe it or not, there is a statute of limitations on debts. It's not that you no longer owe the money after a certain amount of time. The only way to really get rid of a legitimate debt is to pay it off or declare bankruptcy. But under provincial and federal law, most creditors have only a

limited amount of time—typically between two and six
years in which they can sue you to collect. This means that
once any particular debt of yours ages past the deadline, it
becomes effectively uncollectible—and you are effectively
off the hook.

The legal term for this is "time-barred debt."

A time-barred debt is any debt that has been past due for
longer than the applicable statute of limitations. You still owe
the money, but there is nothing your creditor can legally do to
force you to pay it. So with this in mind, what you want to do
is look at all your debts and see if any of them are time-barred.
If they are, you can relax. Practically speaking, you no longer
have to worry about them.

I should add a word of caution here before you think you
can avoid paying your debts if you wait long enough. Banks,
credit card companies, mortgage lenders, and other sources
of loans are not stupid. They pay attention to the statutes of
limitations applicable in all provinces, and they understand
exactly what they have to do to make sure you don't escape
your responsibilities.

MAKE SURE YOU KNOW WHEN
THE CLOCK STARTED TICKING

Once you know what type of debt you have and what statute
of limitations applies, you need to figure out when the deadline clock started ticking. Generally speaking, the countdown
begins when you violate your loan agreement—usually the
first time you miss a payment deadline. But that's not a hard-
and-fast rule. If you make any kind of payment later on or
charge something to the account or do anything that shows

you recognize that you owe the debt, the clock will stop and reset to zero.

Under these circumstances, the countdown would start over again on the account's "date of last activity." For a credit card debt, this would most likely be the last time you used the card or made a payment.

JUST BECAUSE THEY CAN'T SUE YOU DOESN'T MEAN THEY WON'T TRY

Even though a creditor can't take you to court to collect a time-barred debt, that doesn't mean he or she will give up. There are a number of wrinkles in the law, and determined debt collectors try to exploit them. For instance, debtors are covered only by the statute of limitations of the province in which they currently live, not where they originally borrowed the money. So if you move from a province such as Alberta, with a short statute of limitations, to a province such as B.C., with a longer one, you could find that what you thought was a time-barred debt isn't one any longer.

And even if you don't move and your debt is clearly time-barred, that doesn't mean your creditor can't still continue to call you up and send you letters demanding payment. Even worse, the outfit you originally borrowed the money from may write the loan off and sell it to a full-time debt collector. In fact, this is almost always what happens with debts you have owed for a long time. Debt collection is a multi-million dollar industry. There are investors, known as vultures, who buy debt from banks and other creditors, hoping that if they can buy your debt for 10 cents on the dollar, collect 20 cents and make a 100% profit before expenses.

Their expenses, by the way, are low. All they do is fill rooms with professional (and sometimes not so professional) cold-callers, who are usually paid minimum wage plus a commission on the debt they manage to collect. These people tend to be pit bulls. Time-barred or not, they will pull out all the stops trying to get you to pay.

The good news is that Consumer Affairs regulations in all provinces protect you from harassment by debt collectors. So do provincial laws such as the *Collection Agencies Act*. Among other things, debt collectors aren't allowed to contact you at inconvenient times, such as before 7 in the morning or after 9 at night, unless you agree to it. They're also not allowed to telephone you at work unless you agree or unless they don't know how to reach you otherwise.

Here's a partial list of what else the law says bill collectors can't do. (You can find a full list online at **www.consumer-badcreditguide.com/collectionrightscanada.html**.)

- Debt collectors aren't allowed to harass or abuse you. This includes:
  - ▸ Using threats of violence or harm
  - ▸ Using obscene or profane language
  - ▸ Driving you crazy with repeated phone calls

- Debt collectors aren't allowed to lie to you. This includes:
  - ▸ Falsely claiming that they are lawyers or government representatives
  - ▸ Falsely claiming that you have broken the law
  - ▸ Falsely claiming they work for a credit-reporting company
  - ▸ Misrepresenting how much you owe
  - ▸ Falsely claiming you will be arrested if you don't pay your debt

> ▸ Falsely claiming that they'll seize your property or gar-
>   nish your wages unless they are permitted by law to do
>   this and actually intend to do so

- Debt collectors aren't allowed to give false credit information about you to anyone, including a credit-reporting
  company.

- Debt collectors aren't allowed to use a false company name
  or send you anything that looks like an official document
  from a court or government agency if that's not what it
  really is.

- Debt collectors aren't allowed to engage in unfair practices.
  These include:
  - ▸ Making you pay any additional money (whether in the
    form of interest, fees, or special charges) that's not speci-
    fied in your original loan agreement
  - ▸ Depositing a post-dated cheque early
  - ▸ Contacting you by postcard

And while the law does not prohibit anyone from trying to
collect time-barred debts, as long as they do not sue or
threaten to sue you, it does give you the ability to make them
leave you alone.

HOW TO GET A DEBT COLLECTOR OFF YOUR BACK

Amazingly enough, there is a really simple way to stop debt
collectors from bugging you to repay a time-barred debt, even
though you do legally owe the money. All you have to do is

send them a letter telling them to stop contacting you by phone and telling them to contact you only by mail. Once you tell them that (in writing, of course), you may receive a lot of mail, but you won't have to open it and you won't have to listen to the phone ringing every night before 9 and every morning after 7.

You can get more information about debt collection agencies and how to deal with them from Canada's Office of Consumer Affairs, part of Industry Canada (**www.ic.gc.ca**). You'll not only find tips on dealing with these agencies, but also find links to the regulations and guidelines of each province.

DON'T MAKE THIS MISTAKE— IT CAN RESTART THE CLOCK!

One thing you should never do when you're dealing with a creditor regarding a time-barred debt is agree to a payment plan or actually make a payment. Doing this—or anything else that in effect acknowledges that you owe them money— can reset or restart the statute of limitations clock!

This is often the ultimate scam that debt collectors use. They call you up, get you to admit that this debt is yours, and then ask you sign up for a debt repayment plan that might require you to pay as little as 20 cents on the dollar of what you owe. It may sound good in theory, but it can backfire big time. This is because if your debt has already passed the "point of no return," there is no legal action the debt collector can take to make you pay any of it. However, if you agree to a payment plan, the statute of limitations clock starts ticking all over again—which means they can go to court and get a judgment against you.

I recently worked with a woman named Jennifer who owed $30,000 in past-due credit card debt. A debt collector offered to reduce her obligation to just $5,000 if she wired him a cheque in that amount immediately.

Sound like a good deal? Guess again. Jennifer lived in a jurisdiction where there was nothing the debt collector could do legally to force her to pay any of that debt anymore. Most importantly, the debt collector who was harassing her knew this! The debt had already been charged off by the credit card company and the debt collector was nothing more than a vulture who bought her debt for pennies on the dollar.

So what Jennifer did was wrote the debt collector a letter pointing out that the alleged debt was time-barred in her province, and so could the collector please stop bothering her about it.

As a result of this one letter, the collector never called her again.

DEBT COLLECTORS ARE NOT YOUR FRIENDS— DON'T GET SUCKED IN

While some debt collectors come down on you like a ton of bricks, others are more subtle. Instead of trying to intimidate you into paying a time-barred debt, they will attempt to sweet-talk you into cooperating. One common tactic is to offer to give you extra time to pay off the debt or to suggest that you make a small "token payment" just to prove you're a good guy. Don't be taken in.

As I noted earlier, **doing anything to acknowledge that you owe the money—especially agreeing to a payment plan or actually making a payment—can reset or restart the statute of limitations clock.** And that would allow a creditor to get a judgment against you, which could leave you with your bank accounts seized or your wages garnished.

So if you have any time-barred debt, the only response you should have to a creditor's demand for payment is a polite, "Thanks for calling, but I can't help you" along the lines I suggested above.

Another possible response is to say to them, "PROVE IT TO ME. Send me written documentation that proves I owe this money."

The great truth is that many of the collection agencies that call you don't have any proof (and they know it). All they generally have is a long list of names and numbers that they've purchased from a bank or other lender that has given up trying to receive repayment. They don't actually have any proof of the debt, such as copies of the loan agreement you may have signed.

Many lawyers who help people with time-barred debt generally advise clients who have debts that are not yet time-barred but are close to reaching the statute of limitations to lay low and don't do or say anything in response to a creditor that could be construed as admitting you owe the money. Remember, time is on your side, and the vultures who bought your debt from the credit card companies that wrote off your debt know this, which is why they might illegally harass you. Don't let them!

DEBT IS A RIGHTS ISSUE—AND YOU HAVE RIGHTS!

Let me say that I believe in living a life of integrity. When you borrow money, you should pay it back. You made a promise to do just that, and you should always keep your promises. That said, I'm also your advocate. If you owe a debt that your province's statute of limitations defines as "time-barred," you deserve to know your rights. What's more, you are entitled to use those rights to get out of debt and get back on your feet financially.

I'm also enough of a realist to know that much of the money that debt collectors try to collect these days isn't what was originally borrowed. It's sometimes the result of outrageous interest and nonsense fees that were tacked on later. I worked with one couple who had borrowed about $10,000 on their credit card—and had made $14,000 in payments. Nonetheless, what with interest and penalties, they still owed more than $25,000. Now that's just wrong. So I say—use your rights!

LAST BUT NOT LEAST

If your debt isn't time-barred and you can't use this little-known legal right, don't fear—this book contains plenty of other strategies you can use to crush your debt and live Debt Free for Life. So keep reading—and don't forget this strategy just because it may not apply to you. Share it with friends if they are being hounded by creditors. You could wind up saving them a fortune.

YOU DON'T HAVE TO DO IT YOURSELF

As I said before, I believe that just about everything I have suggested in this book, from understanding your rights with time-barred debt to DOLPing your way to financial freedom, is stuff you can do yourself. That said, I have plenty of readers and friends who would rather not do this on their own—who feel more comfortable working with a professional.

A very close friend of mine, who owed more than $100,000 in credit card debt and was just weeks away from bankruptcy, knew he couldn't do it himself. But instead of getting depressed, he went to a non-profit credit-counselling group. The organization saved his life financially. Today, he is completely debt free!

My friend's story is not unusual. Millions of people have gone this route with similar results. So with this in mind, let's look at how these groups work and how to choose one if doing it yourself isn't right for you.

DEBT FREE FOR LIFE ACTION STEPS

❏ *Before you do anything in this chapter, consult a lawyer.*
❏ Check out the statute of limitations on unpaid debts in your province.
❏ Check to see if you have any debts that have been past due for longer than the applicable statute of limitations.
❏ If you do, figure out when the "deadline clock" started ticking.
❏ Instruct—in writing—any debt collectors trying to get you to pay a time-barred debt to stop bothering you.

CHAPTER ELEVEN

HOW TO GET NON-PROFIT CREDIT COUNSELLING—AND A PROFESSIONAL TO GUIDE YOU OUT OF DEBT

Not everyone has the knowledge and the discipline to get out of debt by themselves. Many people—maybe you're one of them—need someone to take them by the hand and walk them out of debt. There is nothing wrong with this.

So if, after reading this book and trying my DOLP Method, you don't feel you can do this by yourself, or you simply don't want to do it yourself, by all means get someone to help you. Just keep in mind that you need to find the right person. That's where this chapter comes in.

My recommendation, if you decide you need some outside help, I recommend that you consider working with a non-profit credit-counselling agency. It may take a little extra effort to find a good one, but it's not that hard and the benefits can be enormous. As I'll share in a moment, my best friend Bob did just that—and in less than five years with the help of a non-profit credit counsellor, he freed himself from more than $100,000 in credit card debt! And he's not alone.

THOUSANDS OF PEOPLE TURN TO NON-PROFIT CREDIT COUNSELLING AGENCIES EVERY YEAR

According to Credit Counselling Canada, more than 150,000 people in Canada have obtained counselling on managing their debts in the last five years. Their average debt was about $25,600, and they owed that money to an average of five different creditors. So if you are reading this book and need help—trust me, there's no reason to be embarrassed. You've got plenty of company.

In this chapter I will explain how non-profit credit counselling works and how it can help you. Among other things, I will cover the following:

- What is non-profit credit counselling?

- What exactly does a non-profit credit counsellor do for you?

- How do you go about finding a non-profit credit counsellor you can trust?

- What are the costs associated with non-profit credit counselling?

I hope you noticed that whenever I refer to credit counselling, I also use the word "non-profit." That's because I want to emphasize that what I'm talking about here *isn't* the for-profit "Debt Settlement" industry. We'll deal with the for-profit companies later, in Chapter Twelve. This chapter is solely about non-profit credit counsellors—and non-profit credit counselling is completely different from the for-profit version.

I do not recommend that you use (or even consider) for-profit credit counselling UNTIL you have already tried non-profit credit counselling.

GOING FROM A SIX-FIGURE CREDIT CARD DEBT
TO BEING DEBT FREE

I mentioned above that a good friend of mine got out from under more than $100,000 in credit card debt by working with a non-profit credit counselling agency. It's a true story. My friend's name is Bob, and just a few days before I wrote this chapter, he and I celebrated his "Debt Freedom Day"—his making the final payment that took care of the last of his credit card debt. Here's what he said to me after he put the cheque in the mail: "David, I now feel like Superman. It's amazing what being out of debt can do for your spirit and your energy."

Considering that five years earlier Bob was considering bankruptcy and feeling totally defeated, his success story is truly AMAZING.

Indeed, Bob's experience was so amazing that it made me see the credit counselling industry in a totally new light. Before I saw Bob turn his life around with the help of a non-profit credit counsellor, I was skeptical of the industry. I had heard too many horror stories about people who had been victimized by debt counsellors and it was hard to really know whom you could trust. But Bob's experience—and that of many others like him—changed my mind.

As I said, Bob and I are best friends. We met in grade school and went all the way through high school together. We have the kind of friendship where you feel like you're family. So I usually knew everything that was going on with Bob, including the fact that he was having great success at work and earning a six-figure salary.

So imagine my shock, on a crisp morning at breakfast with Bob, when he broke down and told me he was in big trouble. In truth, I never would have guessed the problem would be debt. As I said, I was under the impression that Bob was doing really well at work. But that morning Bob told me what was really happening: His business had slowed down, his spending hadn't—and he now owed SIX FIGURES in credit card debt. He had already refinanced his home multiple times and borrowed from his retirement savings plan.

To say he was in deep financial trouble was an understatement. He was literally down to his last few thousand dollars.

HIS INCOME HAD DROPPED, BUT HIS SPENDING HADN'T

Considering that I hear stories like this every day from readers—not to mention people on the street who recognize me from television—Bob's news shouldn't have come as a shock. But I hadn't seen the signs. Bob and I spent a lot of time together. We ate out together, travelled together, shopped together. And then it hit me. Of course I hadn't seen the signs. Bob's behaviour hadn't changed. What had changed was something I had no knowledge about—his income. His income had dropped, but his spending hadn't.

As Bob explained the details, I knew there wouldn't be any quick fix here. I told him over coffee that I thought he could get out of this mess without having to declare bankruptcy, but he would need to get brutally serious about his situation—and he would need to act quickly. "I can give you my tools," I said to him, "but I think you're going to need more help than that. I think you will need to find a non-profit credit counsellor." The challenge, I added, would be finding the right counsellor.

As we parted company that morning, I asked Bob how long

it had taken him to rack up his debt. Bob said it had been about three years.

"Then you should assume it will take you at least three years—and maybe more—to get out," I said. "But if you are committed, you *will* get out—and the time will go by faster than you can imagine."

Bob *was* committed, and things turned out just as I had hoped they would. He found a terrific non-profit credit counselling agency, which renegotiated the terms of his debts with his creditors and got him into a debt management plan. Every month without fail, he sent the agency a chunk of money, which it used to make all his payments. At the same time, he stopped using his credit cards and learned to live on cash and a debit card.

As I type these words, it's amazing to me that five years have passed so quickly since Bob and I had that talk. Today, Bob is out of debt. That's quite the financial turnaround. And I can't take any credit for it. The credit goes completely to Bob (because he committed to changing his life and his spending) and to the non-profit counselling agency (which helped him do what needed to be done).

So now let's see if this could be the right path for you.

WHAT EXACTLY IS NON-PROFIT CREDIT COUNSELLING?

What non-profit credit counselling agencies do is work with you and your creditors to make it possible for you to pay off all your debts—usually within three to five years. They don't reduce the amount you owe, but as was the case with Bob, they can help you develop better financial habits—and, if necessary, they can get your creditors to cut your interest rates and often waive penalty fees, which can bring your monthly payments way down.

What distinguishes non-profit credit counselling agencies from other kinds of debt relief companies is that they are certified by Canada Revenue Agency as being non-profit organizations and registered charities. Most of their expenses are covered by donations from the credit industry itself, which recognizes the value of counselling and debt management. This doesn't mean their services are free—or that earning money isn't important to them. They simply have a different type of financial structure, and the benefit to you the consumer is that it generally costs a lot less to work with them than with a for-profit debt counsellor. If an individual or family cannot pay even a small fee, the non-profit counselling agency will waive its fee altogether.

There are dozens of these non-profit operations throughout Canada. You can find many of them listed on the website of Credit Counselling Canada (**www.creditcounselling-canada.ca**), the Canadian Association of Credit Counselling Services (**www.caccs.c**) and at **www.moneyproblems.ca**.

HOW DO YOU KNOW IF YOU NEED A CREDIT COUNSELLOR?

You may be a good candidate for credit counselling if any or all of the following apply to you.

- After reading this book and putting in place the DOLP Plan, you still feel you could use some hand holding.

- You are having trouble making your monthly minimum payments and you can't consistently pay your bills on time.

- Interest charges are eating you alive, and you've been unable to get the credit card companies to work with you on lowering them.

If any of this sounds familiar, credit counselling may be what you need. With this in mind, let's take a look at exactly what a good non-profit credit counsellor can do for you.

EIGHT WAYS A GREAT NON-PROFIT CREDIT COUNSELLING AGENCY CAN HELP YOU

1. They will offer you a free counselling session.

Before they ask you to sign up for anything, most good non-profit credit counselling agencies will spend at least 60 to 90 minutes with you reviewing your entire debt situation and overall financial position FOR FREE. (Some reputable firms do charge an upfront consultation fee, but it's very small—usually less than $100.) This initial discussion can take place over the phone or in person. But whichever it is, before the counsellor gets into the nuts and bolts of your situation, he or she will probably start with a "holistic approach" to understand your situation better. A common first question is, "What brings you to us today?" This not only helps to break the ice, but also allows the counsellor to really hear your story. The counsellor may then ask you about your goals—what do you really want to accomplish with a debt counsellor? What are your short-term and long-term financial objectives? The idea is to encourage you to think beyond the immediate problem of getting out of debt and start looking forward to a brighter future.

2. They will help you look closely at your financial reality.

Once they have an idea of what brought you to them, a good agency will start evaluating your finances. First, the counsellor will look at what you earn and what your expenses are. Then they will look closely at your debt, how much you owe, what kind of interest rates you are paying, and how much you are wasting in late fees and over-the-limit penalties. Based on all this, the counsellor can figure out if you might be able to get yourself out of debt simply by changing your financial habits or if you need to enroll in what's known as a Debt Management Plan (DMP), where the counsellor negotiates directly with your creditors to work out an arrangement designed to make it possible for you to get out of debt within three to five years.

3. They will create a spending plan or budget for you.

Ultimately, there's no point trying to pay down your debt if you don't—*at the same time*—create a spending plan that allows you to live within your means. Creating this plan or budget is a critical part of what a really good non-profit counsellor will do for you. He or she will study where your money is going and make recommendations about where you can and should cut back in order to live within your means.

> ### 4. They will work with you on "secured debt" as well as credit card debt.

As we discussed earlier, there are two basic forms of debt: secured debt, where you put up collateral (such as a home mortgage or car loan), and unsecured debt, where you don't (most commonly credit card debt). A good counsellor will review both your secured debt and your unsecured debt. If you enroll in a Debt Management Plan, however, it usually will not include secured debts such as a mortgage or car loan, because the creditor can repossess the asset if you fail to make your payments. Ultimately, the counsellor's goal will be first to stabilize your financial life at home—that is, make sure you can buy groceries, keep the lights on, and pay your rent or mortgage. Then he or she will look at the best way to deal with your credit card debt and other unsecured obligations.

> ### 5. They will be prepared to recommend a DMP— but only if it makes sense for you.

Earlier I mentioned the term "Debt Management Plan," or DMP. A DMP is a payment plan that your credit counsellor negotiates with your unsecured creditors to help you get out of debt. Literally thousands of cash-strapped credit card customers have been enrolled in such plans in the last few years.

In most cases, a DMP will do the following:

- It will create a three- to five-year plan to get your debt paid off.

- It will lower the interest rate on your debt—usually to below 10% and sometimes much lower. I have coached people who had their interest rates cut from 29% to *zero* as a result of enrolling in a DMP.

- It will get your credit card company to stop charging you the over-the-limit fees, annual membership fees, and late-payment penalties.

- It will freeze your credit card accounts (meaning you can't use your cards anymore) until your balances have been paid off. Some credit card companies will actually close your account and make you apply for a new card once your debt is paid off.

A reputable non-profit organization won't recommend a DMP to just anyone. On average, about one out of every four people who comes to a credit counsellor is able to sustain a DMP. The fact is that a DMP can't really help you if your debt is so large—or your income is so low—that even after your interest rates were lowered and your penalty fees waived, you still couldn't afford to make your payments. In general, a DMP works for people with debts of $5,000 or less to five or fewer unsecured creditors and who can afford to repay the debt but simply need more time to do it without accumulating more interest. That's why it's critical to have a counsellor who will really look closely at your overall financial situation before making any recommendations.

> ## 6. They will level with you if they think you may need to file for bankruptcy.

In some cases, credit counselling clients probably should consider bankruptcy. (We'll cover the ins and outs of bankruptcy and how to find a good bankruptcy lawyer in Chapter Thirteen.) A good credit counselling agency will let you know right away if this is your situation. To file for bankruptcy in Canada, you must work with a licensed trustee. If your situation requires it, a good counselling agency may provide a list of qualified trustees, bankruptcy lawyers, and legal resources, but will not push you to use any particular one.

> ## 7. They will be able to provide you with references and testimonials.

Most reputable non-profit credit counsellors take great pride in the success stories of their customers—and they should be ready and willing to provide you with references from people like you whom they have helped. If you're considering a credit counselling agency that wasn't recommended to you by someone you know, ask them for the names of three former clients whose situations were similar to yours who might be willing to talk to you about their experiences. You may also want to check with your local Better Business Bureau to see if any complaints have been lodged against the credit counselling agency.

8. They will happily explain their fees upfront.

Any honest, accredited non-profit credit counselling agency will be happy to explain exactly how much they charge—and to put it in writing. As I noted earlier, many won't charge you anything for the first appointment, and those that do generally ask for less than $100. You may have to pay a monthly fee if you enter a DMP, but this too should be nominal—usually $50 a month or less, sometimes nothing at all. If you can't afford to pay, most non-profit consumer counselling organizations will still work with you. In fact, consumers cannot be denied service based on inability to pay.

WHAT A GOOD NON-PROFIT
CREDIT COUNSELLING AGENCY WON'T DO

- The counsellor won't pressure you to sign up with the agency.

- The agency won't charge you a huge sign-up fee. (It shouldn't be more than $100.)

- The agency won't charge you a huge fee each month. (In most cases, it should be $50 or less.)

- The counsellor won't tell you to stop making your monthly credit card or other debt payments so they can negotiate a better deal for you.

- The counsellor won't tell you they can sue the credit card company on your behalf.

- The counsellor won't recommend that you enroll in a DMP before they have taken a good look at your overall financial picture.

HOW NON-PROFIT COUNSELLING AGENCIES
MAKE MONEY

If you're at all like me, you may be wondering how exactly non-profit credit counselling agencies are able to provide all the services they do at such a low cost to the consumer—and often at no cost at all?

The answer isn't simple—but it is important to know. Non-profit credit counselling agencies in Canada primarily receive their funding from credit lenders—that is, the folks to whom you owe the money. Every year they make what are called "fair share contributions" to the agencies. To put it another way, they pay the credit counselling agency a percentage of the debt that the agency helps them to settle. These contributions amount to something under 10% of the total debt repaid. When you consider that in 2009 NFCC member organizations helped to pay down nearly $175 million in consumer credit card debt, that's a lot of money. And the fact is, the arrangement does benefit everyone: consumers get out of debt, creditors get paid back, and the counsellors are able to provide a vital service at a low cost.

FIVE SUPER-SIMPLE STEPS TO FINDING
A GREAT NON-PROFIT CONSUMER
CREDIT COUNSELLING AGENCY

> ### 1. Look for an agency that is a member
> ### of one of the major trade associations.

The best way to ensure that a non-profit credit counselling organization is truly trustworthy is to ensure it is affiliated with the Canadian Association of Credit Counselling Services. This organization requires counsellors to meet minimum training standards and adhere to a code of ethical practices. Check with the organizations directly to confirm whether an agency is in fact a member.

Canadian Association of Credit Counselling Services
www.caccs.ca
(800) 263-0260
The Canadian Association of Credit Counselling Services (CACCS) represents a Canada-wide network of accredited, non-profit agencies and affiliates offering preventive education and confidential services to clients experiencing financial difficulties.

With a focus on financial counselling education, accreditation of agencies, and certification of Credit Counsellors, CACCS is also committed to national research and policy initiatives concerning personal finance and industry advocacy.

Credit Counselling Canada
www.creditcounsellingcanada.ca
(866) 398-5999

Credit Counselling Canada (CCC) is the national association of not-for-profit credit counselling and government agencies that work provincially, regionally, and locally throughout Canada. Only not-for-profit registered charitable organizations are accepted as association members by our Board of Directors.

This common bond of charitable, not-for-profit status ensures that all member activities remain focused on assisting those in need by providing timely and useful help. This commitment is also reflected in their independent accreditation process, which requires adherence to the highest standard of service.

---

2. Ask the right questions when you first meet with them.

When you sit down and go through your initial counselling session with a non-profit credit counsellor, you should ask the following questions.

- Are you a non-profit organization recognized by the CRA? (The answer must be yes, and the counsellor should provide you with proof.)

- What licences do you have?

- How are your people trained and are they certified debt counsellors?

- How long have you been doing this? What training do you have? (You want to work with someone who has experience and isn't a brand new hire.)

- What is the counselling process like? How long will the first appointment take? What must I do to prepare?

- What happens after that? Will you provide a plan in writing for me?

- If you take over my bill paying as part of a DMP, when exactly will you disburse payments to my creditors? (It should be at least twice a month.) Will you provide me with proof of payment and written progress reports? If so, how often?

- Will the money I send you as part of a DMP be protected and, if so, how?

- Do you offer any ongoing educational programs that will help me become smarter about getting and staying out of debt.

- What will counselling cost me—and will you put it in writing?

3. Interview more than one agency.

I'm a huge believer in the importance of doing your homework. After all, you don't know what you don't know until you do. So before you sign up with anyone, make a point of interviewing at least two or three different agencies. In addition to learning about how they work, you want to see if the personal "chemistry" is right. This may seem like a lot of work, but it's important that you feel really comfortable and confident about the agency you select because you will likely be working with the counsellors for years.

> ## 4. Check out the agency with the Better Business Bureau.

Go to the Better Business Bureau website (**www.bbb.org/Canada**) and check to see if the agency you're considering is a member—and, if so, whether there have been any complaints filed against it. Even though I happen to know many excellent non-profit credit counselling agencies that don't belong to the Better Business Bureau, I still think it's worth checking the BBB website. I would also Google the name of any agency you are considering along with the word "complaints" to see if anything comes up.

> ## 5. Get referrals and references.

Referrals from trusted sources are always a great way to go. So ask your friends and co-workers as well as any professionals you may work with (such as accountants or lawyers) if they happen to know of a GREAT non-profit credit counselling organization in your area. The idea of asking about credit counselling may strike you as embarrassing, but it's time to stop being embarrassed and start taking action. If you can't get a personal referral, get the names of several agencies in

your area from the CACCS or Credit Counselling Canada—
and then ask the agencies for references or testimonials from
people like you whom they have helped. And then call those
former clients and get their feedback on their experience.

Now that we've learned how the non-profit consumer credit
counselling world works and what it can do for you, let's take
a look at the "for-profit" debt-reduction business, otherwise
known as the debt settlement industry. As I said at the beginning of the book, this is a world filled with pitfalls, so it's
important to know what to watch out for.

DEBT FREE FOR LIFE ACTION STEPS

❏ Decide if you're a good candidate for credit counselling.
❏ If you are, check with one of the umbrella counselling
  groups for a member agency in your area.
❏ Come to your initial meeting, prepared to question the
  counsellor about his or her credentials, how he or she
  works, and what (if anything) the service will cost.
❏ Interview more than one agency, check all of them out
  with the Better Business Bureau, and ask for referrals
  and references.

CHAPTER TWELVE

DEBT SETTLEMENT: SOLUTION OR SCAM?

If it sounds too good to be true—it probably is too good to be true!

The debt settlement industry has developed a bad reputation. In the United States, a consumer protection bill is being considered that would radically change the way this industry operates. In Canada, credit counsellors and bankruptcy experts caution people to make sure they know exactly what they're doing before they agree to a debt settlement plan. While the U.S. debt settlement industry deserves its questionable reputation, many people say the Canadian industry is more reputable. What's true in both countries is that people with serious debt problems are desperate and vulnerable, and they may jump at any opportunity to get themselves out of difficulty, even if it seems too good to be true.

In any case, you need to know the facts about what debt settlement is and what it isn't. So let's get started!

THE DEBT SETTLEMENT GAME— WHAT YOU NEED TO KNOW

"Get Out of Debt with One Monthly Payment! Reduce Your Debt up to 50%!"

"Are you behind on your credit card bills, need cash to pay your debt off—call us we can help you cut your debt in half in minutes!"

"If We Can't Get You Out of Debt in 24 Hours, We'll Pay You $100!"

You've seen these ads, haven't you? Of course you have. They are everywhere—on television and radio, in newspapers and magazines, online in banner ads and mock advertorials. And the reason you and I are seeing these ads is because they are effective. People are calling.

But does any of what they promise actually work?

And what exactly are they promising?

According to them, debt settlement companies act on behalf of consumer debtors to help them clear their debts. They do this by entering into direct negotiations with creditors in order to facilitate the repayment of debts. They also refer to their operations as "a bankruptcy prevention program" that "provides financial freedom without the long-term affects [sic] that come with bankruptcy."

In plain English, this means that they will pick up the phone and call a credit card company on your behalf. Say you owe $10,000 on your Scotiabank Visa and have fallen behind on your payments. The debt settlement company might call up Scotiabank and ask if they would be willing to settle what you owe in return for an immediate cash payment of $5,000. Operating on the theory that something is usually better than nothing, Scotiabank would probably at least consider the offer.

Of course, if you're like most people who owe too much on their credit cards, you probably don't have $5,000 in cash to pay. So in most cases the debt settlement company will suggest that you start sending it some money each month, which it will hold in a savings account. When the balance starts approaching $5,000, staff will give the credit card company a call and see if they can make a deal.

Hmmmm. Doesn't this sound like something you could do yourself without having to pay anyone any fees or take any risk?

HOW DEBT SETTLEMENT OFTEN REALLY WORKS

Actually, the debt settlement strategy I just described is quite logical. But that doesn't mean it always works.

For starters, many creditors refuse to work with debt settlement companies. So regardless of how good a debt settlement company says it is, if you have debt with, say, American Express, there won't be anything the company can do to help you. Why? Because as of this writing, American Express has a blanket policy of not working with for-profit debt settlement companies. As American Express spokeswoman Marina Hoffman Norville explained it, *"We believe there is no service or benefit that a for-profit debt-settlement company can offer our card members that they could not receive from working directly with us."* So before you even consider working with a debt settlement company, it pays to check whether your credit card company will even talk to the company.

On top of this, working with a debt settlement company often creates immediate additional problems for you. Chances are that one of the first things they will suggest is that you stop making payments on the debt you're hoping to settle. If you ask why, they will offer what sound like two good reasons. For one thing, not paying your bills will allow you to send more money to the debt settlement company, which in turn will make your settlement fund grow more quickly. For another, as long as you continue to make payments, your creditor won't have any reason to settle your debt. Again, this is logical but not practical. The problem is that this approach can quickly destroy what's left of your financial life. Not paying a creditor you can afford to pay opens you to a world of hurt. The moment you fall behind on your payments, interest and penalty charges will begin to accrue, making your total debt even bigger. It will also immediately lower your credit score, which will make it even harder to refinance any of your debt. Even worse, many lenders routinely turn over debts that aren't being paid to collection agencies or lawyers, who may in turn sue you for payment.

The industry insists that reputable debt settlement firms don't tell people to stop paying their bills, but countless reporters and commentators who have tested these claims have determined that they do. For example, a bankruptcy trustee named Douglas Hoyes tells a story on the Bankruptcy Canada website (**www.bankruptcy-canada.ca**) about a client with $27,000 in credit card debt to three different card companies. He paid $300 a month to a debt management company for 11 months. Two of the companies didn't bother him, but the third company took him to court and garnished his wages. This would have made it impossible for him to continue setting aside the $300 monthly payments, so he consulted Hoyes and filed a consumer proposal.

We'll talk about consumer proposals in more detail in Chapter Thirteen. In the meantime, all you need to know is that a consumer proposal would have made this client's life easier if he'd filed it in the first place instead of setting up a debt management plan. As Hoyes says, "A consumer proposal, once accepted by a majority of creditors, is legally binding on all unsecured creditors. A debt management plan isn't."

YOUR DEBT MAY ACTUALLY RISE

The fact is that even debt management companies themselves admit that in most cases working with a debt settlement company will cause your debt to increase. A typical debt settlement client will see the amount he owes go up by an average of 20% over the two or three years that the settlement process generally takes. That's because the debts usually continue to accumulate interest as the client squirrels away his monthly payments under his debt management plan. At the same time, as your debt falls increasingly past due, your credit score will suffer. And before too long, you may start getting anxiety-producing phone calls from collection agents.

Debt management companies insist that, if you stick with the program, the chances are good that all your debts will end up being settled for less than 50 cents on the dollar. There are lots of reasons not to believe this, and we'll get into that later, but even when a debt settlement program works, it can still cause you trouble.

HURTING YOUR CREDIT SCORE—
AND INCREASING YOUR TAX BILL

As I noted above, if you stop making payments on accounts, as many settlement firms suggest, your credit rating will immediately take a hit. According to FICO, stopping payments to creditors as part of a debt settlement program can shave anywhere between 65 to 125 points from your credit score. What's more, if you wind up settling a debt for less than you owe, it will likely be reported to the credit bureaus *not* as "paid in full" or "paid as agreed" (both of which make you look good) but as "settled for less than full balance." Lenders hate to see this, and it will do terrible damage to your FICO score.

And once your debt is settled, that is *not* the end of it. A debt settlement is considered a negative event, and negative events stay on your credit report, affecting your credit score, for up to seven years.

Debt settlements also have tax implications. If you settle a debt to a financial institution like a bank or credit card company for less than you owe, the amount you don't have to pay (technically known as a "discharge of indebtedness") is generally considered by Canada Revenue Agency as taxable income—meaning you're going to wind up owing the government some money.

IT'S NOT CHEAP AND THERE RARELY ARE REFUNDS

Finally, the debt settlement process is not cheap. As a rule, the fee you're charged depends on the size of the debt you want the company to settle for you. Debt management companies say their fees depend on the size of the debt, but in general they charge an average of 15% to 18% of a client's enrolled debt over three years, plus a service fee that might run $25 or $50 a month. (So if you're hoping to have them settle $10,000 in debt, you're probably looking at a total cost of around $2,000.) Keep in mind, though, that some companies may charge more than others.

Many companies make you pay the fee in advance, and

they generally keep it all whether or not they settle all your debts. There are a few debt settlement firms that operate on a contingency basis, meaning you have to pay only if they come through for you, but they charge a much higher percentage— as much as 35% of the settled debt amount.

Typically, at least part of the monthly payment you make to a debt settlement company goes to pay your fee. Most firms will spread out the cost over a year or longer—deducting, say, $100 a month from your payment for 18 months. But some like to grab their entire portion upfront. It's not unknown, for example, for clients to make sizable payments for as long as four months before a single cent is credited to their debt settlement fund. Even worse, desperate people may make payments for far longer than that—forking over tens of thousands of dollars in the process—and get nothing at all for their trouble except a ruined credit rating and even bigger debts than they started out with.

In one case, a couple, overwhelmed by credit card debt and desperate to avoid bankruptcy, agreed to pay a debt settlement company $1,700 a month. Seven months later, having paid in more than $11,000, the wife called the company to check on where things stood. She was told they had accrued only $3,000 in savings and none of their credit card debts had been settled. The couple immediately withdrew from the program, but the damage was done. Since they had stopped making payments to their creditors, their total debt had ballooned and they were now receiving collection notices and threats of lawsuits. In the end, they wound up having to declare bankruptcy.

WHEN DEBT SETTLEMENT MIGHT MAKE SENSE

So should you—or anyone—ever use a debt settlement company? Personally, I wouldn't let anyone I love go this route. But there are some narrow circumstances when using one might make sense.

To begin with, debt settlement is something you should consider only if your debt problems mainly involve credit cards and other unsecured debt. If you're also struggling to keep the bank from foreclosing on your mortgage, you should concentrate on that. Saving your home is more important than paying off your credit cards.

Keep in mind, too, that whether you are doing the negotiating or some company is negotiating for you, certain kinds of debt are more likely to be settled than others. The best bets for settlement are:

- Debts owned by third parties. If your debt has been sold, the company that bought it almost certainly paid less than face value and will be highly motivated to settle.

- Debts that are so far past due that they are close to being written off by the lender.

USE THE DEBT-SETTLEMENT CHECKLIST

Here's a simple checklist you can use to help you decide whether debt settlement is right for you. If you can check off all of the boxes, the answer may be yes.

❏ I have sufficient income to pay my living expenses and still be able to repay at least 40% of my debt over the next three years.
❏ I have already tried negotiating my debts directly with the credit card issuer or other creditor without success.
❏ I understand that the process may not work and that my credit will be hurt.
❏ I am emotionally prepared to deal with creditors' phone calls.
❏ I have thoroughly checked out any debt-settlement company I am considering, including reading the Better Business Bureau report on it and talking to others who have used it.

FINDING THE RIGHT
DEBT SETTLEMENT COMPANY

That last item in the checklist is crucial. The chances of running into a scam artist in the debt settlement industry are unfortunately very high, and you're asking for trouble if you don't check out a company thoroughly before you sign up with it.

What should you look for? For starters, go to the Better Business Bureau website (**www.bbb.org/Canada**) and run a search on the company you're considering. If you find they have hundreds of complaints and an "F" rating, then run from them. (This may sound obvious—but you'd be amazed how many people don't do this.)

Here are a number of helpful tips for finding a reputable debt-settlement provider. Among the highlights:

- A reputable company will always discuss the potential challenges as well as the benefits of its debt settlement program before enrolling you as a client.

- A reputable company will provide a written explanation of its cancellation or refund policy.

- A reputable company will display the street address of its main office on its website.

- A reputable company will conduct a thorough review of your financial situation including all expenses and income before determining whether you are eligible for its debt settlement program.

- A reputable company will provide you with a copy of its service agreement before asking you for banking information, accounting information, or your Social Insurance Number.

- Above all, you should shop around and compare.

FOR WHAT IT'S WORTH

All things being equal (which at this point they are, if you haven't yet started this process), I suggest that before you consider debt settlement, you first try my DOLP method to get out of debt. If this approach doesn't work for you, or you feel you need someone to help you with it, look for a non-profit credit counselling organization.

Only after you've exhausted all these options should you perhaps approach a debt settlement company. And then make sure you do with your eyes wide open and your questions ready from the list I provided in this chapter.

Okay, my friend—we've made a ton of progress on your Debt Free for Life education and journey. Now let's take a look at an alternative that I personally regard as an absolute last resort, but something you need to know about anyway—the ins and outs of personal bankruptcy.

DEBT FREE FOR LIFE ACTION STEPS

- ❏ Use the Debt Settlement Checklist to decide whether or not debt settlement is right for you.
- ❏ Make sure your creditors don't have a policy of refusing to deal with debt settlement companies.
- ❏ Shop around, check with the Better Business Bureau, and ask for referrals and references.
- ❏ Before you turn over any personal information or sign any contracts, get a copy of the company's service agreement and cancellation or refund policy.

CHAPTER THIRTEEN

HOW BANKRUPTCY WORKS, WHEN TO USE IT, HOW LONG IT WILL TAKE YOU TO RECOVER

This is a chapter I hope you will never need to use. But even if you don't, you may know someone who isn't so lucky.

As I write this, total insolvencies, which include actual bankruptcies and proposals (we'll discuss these later in this chapter), were down in 2010. But in 2009, almost 116,000 Canadians either declared bankruptcy or filed a proposal to creditors. That was an increase of more than 30% over 2008 and was a sure sign that Canadians were hurting as the recession took its toll. In fact, since the recession started in 2008, not a week goes by that someone doesn't ask me, "David, should I declare bankruptcy?"

My answer is always the same: *If you think you may need to declare bankruptcy, get yourself some professional financial and legal advice* TODAY. The number-one complaint I hear from bankruptcy trustees and lawyers is that most people come to them too late—and as a result they can't protect any of their assets in court because they've already gone through all of them.

Most experts talk about bankruptcy as being a last resort, and I don't disagree. **BUT, if bankruptcy is the right solution for you, the key to making it work is not waiting too long.** The sooner you get professional advice, the sooner the process can help you and the better off you will be. So with this in mind, let's look at what bankruptcy is, who it can help, and whether or not it's right for you or someone you know.

WHAT EXACTLY IS BANKRUPTCY
AND HOW DOES IT WORK?

So what is bankruptcy? According to the definition used by the Office of the Superintendent of Bankruptcy Canada (OSB), "bankruptcy is a legal process carried out through a trustee in bankruptcy designed to relieve honest but unfortunate debtors of their debt burden. When individuals are in bankruptcy, creditors cannot initiate any collection actions against them."

In other words, bankruptcy is a way to wipe out many types of debt and give yourself a fresh start. The very act of filing a bankruptcy petition—that is, asking the OSB for protection under federal bankruptcy law—immediately stops creditors from calling and gives you time to work things out by bringing at least a temporary halt to lawsuits, garnishments, repossessions, foreclosures, and evictions. (What happens is that the OSB-licensed trustee oversees your bankruptcy and informs your creditors that a filing has been made and that by law they can no longer bother you.)

If you complete the bankruptcy process successfully, the trustee will sell all of your qualified assets and hold the proceeds in trust for distribution to your creditors. Bankruptcy does not relieve you of the obligation to pay alimony and child support, payments on a student loan less than seven years old, and fines imposed by the courts. But all or part of your other debts will be erased and your creditors will just have to write them off. It's truly legal magic. Once the OSB has declared a debt of yours discharged, it is gone, disappeared, eradicated— no one can legally make any attempt to make you pay it ever again. You don't even have to pay income taxes on the amount that's wiped out, the way you do when a debt is reduced in a debt settlement.

WHAT YOU NEED TO KNOW
ABOUT INSOLVENCY

Generally speaking, there are two different types of insolvency for individuals: a proposal to creditors and outright bankruptcy. In both cases, you need to work with a trustee in bankruptcy.

PROPOSAL TO CREDITORS

With a proposal to creditors, your trustee interviews you about your financial affairs, including your income, total assets, total debts, and other factors, then assembles an offer to pay creditors a percentage of the debt that you owe them over a specified period. In addition to reducing the total obligation, the trustee might also try to extend the period over which you have to repay your creditors.

Once the trustee files your proposal, you stop making payments directly to your unsecured creditors. Salary garnishments and lawsuits filed against you by creditors will stop, as well.

From the date that the trustee files your proposal, creditors have 45 days to either accept or reject it. Your creditors may call a meeting where each creditor can vote on accepting or rejecting your proposal. Votes are allotted according to the amount of money that you owe to each creditor, and the decision is made by a simple majority.

Once your creditors accept your proposal, you make either a lump-sum payment or periodic payments through your trustee, who then administers the payments to your creditors. The debt must be paid within five years, and your total debt, excluding your principal residence, cannot exceed $250,000. You also have to attend two counselling sessions. As long as you make your payments, you retain ownership of your assets. If you fall more than three months behind in your payments, the proposal becomes null, and your creditors can take action to recover the money that you owe them.

If your creditors do not accept your proposal, you may consider other options for resolving your financial difficulties, including revising your proposal, or declare bankruptcy.

BANKRUPTCY

As I mentioned earlier, bankruptcy, in the words of the OSB, is designed to relieve "honest but unfortunate" debtors of their debt burden. You file for bankruptcy through a trustee.

When you are in bankruptcy, no unsecured creditor can garnish your wages or initiate any other action against you to collect an outstanding debt. Secured creditors, however, are not affected by your bankruptcy status and can still repossess the asset such as a house or a car that you've used to secure your debt.

To declare bankruptcy, a trustee files the required forms on your behalf with the OSB. Once you are declared bankrupt, the trustee deals directly with your creditors. In the meantime, you stop making payments, and salary garnishments and lawsuits filed against you by creditors stop as well.

The trustee then sells your assets, except those that are exempted by law. Depending on the province where you live, these exempted assets might include your principal residence, retirement savings and pensions, food, clothing, some furniture, and a car.

At the same time as the trustee sells your assets, you also have to make payments to the trustee for distribution to your creditors. The trustee determines the amount of these payments, depending on your income and other factors.

After filing for bankruptcy, you may be questioned under oath by an officer of the OSB about your conduct and the causes of your bankruptcy. You'll have to attend two counselling sessions, as well.

If this is your first bankruptcy, you will usually be discharged automatically after nine months. Once that happens, you're released from the obligation to repay your unsecured debts, except for alimony and child support, student loans, court-imposed fines and debt arising from fraud. Some people choose to repay their creditors anyway, once they get back on their feet again.

BANKRUPTCY MAY BE RIGHT FOR YOU, BUT ARE YOU RIGHT FOR BANKRUPTCY?

In order to figure out whether declaring bankruptcy might make sense for you, you need to take into account a number of factors. Basically, it's appropriate to consider bankruptcy if your unsecured debts (such as what you owe from such things as credit cards, uninsured home repairs, and dental bills) are so large that, no matter how much you scrimp and save, there is no way you could repay them within five years.

Of course, bankruptcy may look like a good solution to your debt problems, but that doesn't mean it's the right solution for you. For one thing, there are a series of conditions you have to meet in order to qualify for bankruptcy protection. They include:

- **How much income you earn.** If you earn more than a reasonable amount, based on standards set by the OSB applicable to your situation, you will have to hand over the surplus to the trustee for payment to your creditors.

- **What types of debts you owe.** Some debts cannot be discharged or reduced through bankruptcy. For example, bankruptcy won't help with child support or student loans and it cannot be used to reduce the amount owed on a first mortgage or a new or late-model car.

- **What kind of assets you own.** Many people are able to keep all their assets in bankruptcy. However, some assets are vulnerable, depending on the type of bankruptcy filing and the province where you live.

- **Your future outlook.** Will you be able to pay your bills on time once you emerge from the bankruptcy process? If not, you may want to delay filing. Why go through bankruptcy and then start running up new debts as soon as you get through it? If you think you're looking at more borrowing down the road, it's probably better to hold off on bankruptcy until you're in a position to discharge all your debts at the same time.

Let's look at all these factors in a little more detail.

HOW YOUR INCOME AFFECTS
YOUR BANKRUPTCY RIGHTS

As I noted above, the OSB applies standards to your total family income to see if you should make a monthly payment based on the surplus. The more you earn, the more you have to pay.

If you earn $1,800 a month, for example, and your spouse earns $1,000, you'll be required to make a monthly payment of $146. (You can see how this calculation is made at the website of Bankruptcy Canada, **www.bankruptcycanada.com**).

For a single person, the OSB allows take-home pay (after taxes) of $1,870 a month. If the person earns over $2,070 a month, he or she has to contribute half of the surplus, or $100, each month to what is called "the bankruptcy estate."

Your surplus affects the length of time that you remain in bankruptcy. If it's $200 or less, and it's your first bankruptcy, you usually get a discharge after nine months. If it's more than $200 a month, you remain in bankruptcy for 21 months, and you have to make your surplus income payment for an additional year.

WHAT KIND OF DEBTS CAN BE
WIPED OUT BY BANKRUPTCY

For the most part, bankruptcy allows you to wipe out unsecured debt, such as credit card balances and what you owe from house repairs, dental, or medical bills, drugs, etc. And while it can't wipe out secured debt, it can often make it easier to manage.

As I explained earlier in the section about Debt Management Plans, a secured debt is a debt that is backed up (or guaranteed) by collateral, such as a mortgage secured by your house or a car loan secured by your vehicle. With this type of loan, the debt and the property go together, and bankruptcy can't separate them. If you want to get rid of the debt, you have to give up the property.

Bankruptcy may also be helpful with secured debt when you want to keep an asset. Say you're upside-down on a car loan, but feel you could afford to keep making payments if only the lender would lower your interest rate or give you more time to pay it off. If you're considering bankruptcy or a proposal for creditors, the threat could improve your negotiating stance. After all, if you file for bankruptcy and the car is sold off, your lender will get only a portion of what he's owed—and because of your bankruptcy, he won't be able to collect the difference from you. Rather than run the risk of getting stuck like this, he might be willing to improve the terms of your loan if you agree to keep making payments.

WHAT KIND OF DEBTS CAN'T BE WIPED OUT

In addition to most secured debt, there are some types of unsecured debt that bankruptcy can't erase. These include:

- **Child support and alimony.** Filing for bankruptcy won't get you out of paying alimony or child support, which are classified as domestic support obligations and thus have priority over other types of unpaid debts. That said, it is sometimes possible to reduce divorce-related property settlements through bankruptcy.

- **Student loans.** As a general rule, student loans cannot be discharged if you file for bankruptcy within seven years of completing your studies. The good news here is that there are administrative procedures separate from bankruptcy through which some student loans can be revised or eliminated. (See Chapter Nine for details.)

- **Income taxes.** Canada Revenue Agency can register as a secured creditor against real estate or personal property of a debtor. That means the CRA can seize your house, car or furniture if you don't pay your taxes.

- **Legal judgments against you.** Generally speaking, bankruptcy will not wipe out debts incurred as a result of illegal behaviour on your part. For example, drunk drivers who cause accidents in which someone is injured or killed can't escape the financial consequences of a legal judgment by filing for bankruptcy. Similarly, bankruptcy doesn't affect government fines and penalties, court-ordered restitution, debt related to theft or fraud, and debt related to intentional wrongdoing.

- **Any debts you don't list in your filing.** If you leave it out, it won't be discharged.

HOW MUCH OF YOUR STUFF WILL YOU HAVE TO GIVE UP?

One of the biggest—and most understandable—questions that people ask when they are facing bankruptcy is what it will mean in terms of losing the stuff they own. Will I have to sell my house and my car? What about my retirement accounts? My boat? My jewellery? The family heirlooms I inherited?

Basically, what you can keep and what you must give up when you file for bankruptcy depends on whether the stuff you're worried about keeping is considered an "exempt asset." And the definition of an exempt asset depends on where you live in Canada.

Each province has different ways of conferring exempt status on the belongings of a person who declares bankruptcy. In Ontario, you can keep your pension plan and RRSP; in Alberta, you can't. In Nova Scotia, you can keep a car with a maximum equity value of $6,500 if you need it for your job. This means, if your car is worth $10,000 and you owe $6,000 on it, you can keep the $4,000 in equity and your unsecured creditors can't take that money. The Northwest Territories and Yukon, on the other hand, allow you to retain the equity in a car to a maximum of just $600 and only if it's considered a tool of your trade.

Provinces and territories allow you to keep your principal residence if you declare bankruptcy, but some provinces place a limit on its value. If the value surpasses the limit, you have to sell your house. In Saskatchewan, for example, the limit is $32,000 and associated land up to 160 acres. In Quebec, the limit is $10,000. In Ontario, there's no limit on the value of the personal residence that you can keep, but you'll probably have to hand over the equity in your house to the trustee. A trustee can advise you on whether or not you should keep your house and continue making payments or sell it.

It stands to reason, then, that if you are contemplating filing for bankruptcy, one of the first things you want to do is find out what exemptions are available to you. You can find a summary of each province's bankruptcy exemptions at

www.bankruptcy-canada.ca. But the definitions change frequently, so you really should consult a trustee in bankruptcy before you make any assumptions about what you can and can't keep after you declare bankruptcy.

YOUR RETIREMENT ACCOUNTS CAN BE PROTECTED—BUT NOT IF YOU'VE ALREADY CASHED THEM OUT

This is such an important point that I want you to read this section TWICE. In an effort to pay down their debts, many people in financial trouble pull money out of their retirement accounts before they meet with a non-profit credit counsellor or bankruptcy specialist. Please don't do this. In some provinces, filing for bankruptcy can protect your retirement accounts— but not if you already cashed them out! This is why I almost NEVER recommend cashing out retirement accounts to pay down credit card debts. (In provinces such as B.C. and Alberta, your RRSP and other pension plans aren't exempt anyway.)

On the other hand, the bankruptcy trustee can claim tax refunds, refundable utility deposits, and vacation or leave-of-absence pay that you have coming to you.

WHAT BANKRUPTCY WILL DO TO YOUR CREDIT SCORE

Bankruptcy will definitely hurt your credit rating, but maybe not as much as you think. In fact, once you've gotten through it, you may find that you are more attractive to some lenders than you are now, because you will no longer be burdened by debt. As a result, if you can show that you've learned to handle your finances responsibly, you should be able to get credit again within a year or two of completing a bankruptcy.

Still, a consumer proposal will stay on your credit report for three years. If you default on the proposal, that will stay on your credit report for six years. Bankruptcy remains on your Equifax credit report for six years after the date of discharge and for seven years in your TransUnion report. If you declare bankruptcy more than once, each one remains on your report for fourteen years.

However, even while it's still on your report, the negative impact of a bankruptcy will gradually diminish because credit scoring gives the most weight to recent events.

Any debts discharged through bankruptcy should be listed on your credit report with a balance of zero. Check your report a few months after your discharge to be sure this has happened. If some debts still show a balance, dispute the report with the credit bureau. (See Chapter Seven for instructions on how to do this.) Note that bankruptcy will not erase a history of late payments from your credit report. You may not owe the money anymore, but your inability to pay on time remains a fact that nothing can change.

WHAT NOT TO DO

If you are thinking of filing for bankruptcy, there are certain things that can get you in trouble with the bankruptcy authorities. For example, failing to honestly disclose your assets, even if they are exempt assets, can result in your bankruptcy filing being thrown out by the Office of the Superintendent of Bankruptcy without any of your debts being discharged. It could also result in criminal charges being filed against you. Under the *Bankruptcy and Insolvency Act*, you could be fined as much as $10,000 and spend three years in jail.

Other no-no's include transferring assets to friends or relatives for less than fair market value and paying off debts to family members or favoured creditors.

Basically, anyone who thinks it's possible to game the bankruptcy process is asking for trouble. You need to be totally honest about what you owe and what you have. As one legal expert has said: "The people that work in this field are very good at detecting an avoidance of the truth. There's a much better chance of being caught [cheating in a bankruptcy filing] than being caught cheating on your taxes." And if you are caught trying to get away with something, your bankruptcy will likely be cancelled.

As I said at the beginning of this chapter, you also don't want to put off filing for too long. According to research conducted by the Consumer Bankruptcy Project in the United States, around 40% of those who file bankruptcy take at least two years to decide pull the trigger—by which time many of them have exhausted most of their resources. Experts agree that waiting until your resources are entirely depleted defeats the main point of bankruptcy, which is not to punish people but to help them start over with their financial lives and avoid the mistakes that got them into trouble in the first place.

THE IMPORTANCE OF GETTING EXPERT HELP

Obviously, filing for bankruptcy is not something you should do without giving it considerable thought. Nor can you do it on your own.

Indeed, it is such a big step that the law requires you to complete two counselling courses before you will be granted a bankruptcy discharge. The courses are provided by the trustee in bankruptcy, either one on one or in a group. They take about two hours and cost around $85.

BANKRUPTCY ISN'T FREE

Although it may seem absurd, an individual who declares bankruptcy has to pay a fee for the service. The fee covers filing costs, disbursements, taxes and counselling fees.

In most cases, a bankruptcy costs about $20 a month for the nine months a person remains in bankruptcy, although it can go higher in complicated situations. The fees are usually paid out of money raised from the sale of assets. If you can't pay the fees even after the trustee sells your assets, the OSB will refer you to a trustee who will work on your behalf.

You can get more information at: **www.bankruptcy-canada.com.**

BANKRUPTCY IS A TEMPORARY SOLUTION TO A TEMPORARY PROBLEM!

I want to end this discussion of bankruptcy with the following thought: filing for bankruptcy is perfectly okay. It doesn't mean you're a failure or a terrible person. As I said before, thousands of people declare bankruptcy every year. If you choose to go this route, you will not be alone.

What I find really heart wrenching is that there are people who have committed suicide rather than go bankrupt.

NEVER, EVER let your financial situation convince you that life is not worth living. Bankruptcy is a TEMPORARY solution to a TEMPORARY problem.

The feeling of drowning in debt and not seeing any other way out but bankruptcy can drive a lot of people to the edge. Feeling desperate and depressed is not unusual. Just remember that as bad as things may seem, you *can* change your life. If you are feeling overwhelmed by your debts, please find a good credit counselling agency and sign up today. And don't stop there. If you ever find yourself, even for a moment, considering hurting yourself, STOP and call someone you love. Tell them how you are feeling. If this isn't possible, then pick up a phone and call 911, if your crisis is urgent, or visit **www.suicideprevention.ca**.

Finally, and most important of all, remember these words: "This too shall pass." Believe me, it always does!

DEBT FREE FOR LIFE ACTION STEPS

- ❏ If you think bankruptcy might be the right solution for you, seek professional advice sooner rather than later.
- ❏ Understand what kind of debts would be wiped out by a bankruptcy—and what type wouldn't.
- ❏ If you have the resources, you should consider a consumer proposal as an alternative to bankruptcy.
- ❏ NEVER raid your retirement accounts in an effort to stave off bankruptcy. Get legal advice first!
- ❏ Get yourself expert help, including a credit-counselling course with a non-profit credit-counselling agency.

CHAPTER FOURTEEN

MAKE IT AUTOMATIC!
THE AUTOMATIC MILLIONAIRE 2.0

Getting out of debt—and staying debt free—requires commitment, discipline, and hard work. There are no shortcuts. But there is a way to make the job easier. It's something I've been writing, teaching, and talking about for years now. If you want to succeed, *YOU MUST MAKE YOUR PLAN AUTOMATIC.*

The single most important thing I've learned from working with hundreds of clients as a financial advisor, and now from coaching through my books and seminars, is that the only plans that work are the ones that are automatic! Discipline alone doesn't work. Simply working harder to save money usually doesn't work alone. Discipline and hard work take time, and if your plan requires hundreds of separate actions, month after month, year after year, it will fall by the wayside when the going gets tough. Sure, we'd all like to be prudent and disciplined and thrifty. But how many of us actually are? Over the years, I've had countless clients who insisted they were disciplined enough to do it themselves. In fact, there was only one who was actually able to stick to a financial plan manually (that is, by sitting down and writing himself cheques every month) for any length of time.

The government knows we can't be trusted. That's why it came up with withholding to pay our income tax bills .It knows that the only way to guarantee that you will pay your tax bill is to take the money from your paycheque AUTOMATICALLY before you can spend it.

This is a strategy worth imitating. You need to do for yourself what the government did for itself: set up a system that guarantees you can't spend all your money on other things before you get around to putting your hard-earned dollars where they're supposed to go—to ensuring a richer future. Set it up so that you have to take action only *once*, and you guarantee your success.

Even if you think you're the most disciplined person in the world, don't regard the automatic part as an optional extra. There's a reason it has its own chapter in this book. If you are serious about becoming Debt Free for Life, it's not enough to say you're going to do it. You've also got to make the process automatic.

If you follow the action steps in this chapter you will truly have a foolproof, no-brainer, "set it and forget it" financial plan that, I promise you, will work. The plan is based on the one I laid out my best-seller *The Automatic Millionaire*, but I've updated it for 2011. It will take you less than an hour to get it organized. Read the steps and follow the diagram. It's easy and, YES, YOU REALLY CAN DO IT.

Are you ready?

Then let's go make it automatic!

MAKING IT AUTOMATIC IN LESS THAN AN HOUR

1. Pay yourself first automatically.

In my books, TV and radio appearances, and seminars, I've always emphasized the critical importance of paying yourself first—having at least 5% of what you earn deducted from your paycheque and deposited directly into a registered retirement savings plan. Ideally, this deduction should total 12.5% of your gross income (the equivalent of one hour's worth of work each day). But whatever you can manage, you must make the process automatic. The good news is that you can make these contributions automatic either through your employer or your bank. You just sign up for the program.

If your employer doesn't accommodate automatic payroll deductions, your bank will handle all the arrangements for you, contacting your employer's payroll department on your behalf and dealing with all the paperwork.

And yes, you should do this even if you are in debt! After more than two decades of experience teaching people about money, I have come to believe with all my heart that it's a big mistake to put off saving money until you are debt free. If you do, you may never get started saving. And you'll miss out on the matching contribution many employers offer on group RRSPs. Instead, start by automatically saving a minimum of 5%—or the amount up to which your employer will match— and then gradually increase it to at least 10%.

2. Deposit your paycheque automatically.

If your employer uses a computerized payroll system, you should be able to arrange with your company's personnel or human resources department to have your pay automatically deposited directly into your bank account. This is known as direct deposit. It gets your pay into your account without delay—and saves you the trouble of wasting a lunch hour every week or two waiting in line at the bank with a paper cheque.

3. Fund your emergency account automatically.

I've also long advocated the importance of maintaining an emergency cash cushion of at least three months' worth of expenses in a bank account (*not* your regular chequing account but a separate one set up specially for this purpose). Until this emergency account is fully funded, you should have at least another 5% of your paycheque directly deposited into it. Your bank will do this automatically if you keep your chequing account and your emergency account at the same bank.

4. Pay your credit card bills automatically.

Call all your credit card companies and arrange to have all your bills come due on the same day of the month—ideally, ten days after your paycheque is normally deposited. (Virtually every credit card company will work with you to change your due date if you ask.) Then use your bank's online bill-paying service to automatically make the minimum payment for each of your cards five days before the bill is due. (If your bank doesn't offer free online bill paying, think about switching to one that does.) If you want to pay more than the minimum on any of your cards—and if you follow my DOLP plan, you will—you can write a cheque for the extra amount. Making your minimum payments automatic ensures that you will never miss a payment deadline and get hit with late fees or penalty interest rates.

5. Fund your "extra payments" automatically.

In addition to making all your minimum payments automatically, you should also automate your "extra payments." Based on your DOLP plan you now know which debt should be your #1 priority. If you add just an extra $10 a day to the minimum payment of your #1 debt, that's $300 a month that should be automatically added toward your debt each month. Arrange to have this amount (or whatever amount you've decided on) transferred automatically from your chequing account to the appropriate loan account until it's paid off. Once you have automated this debt down to nothing, you should automate your #2 debt. And so on—until all of your debts are paid off completely. The same goes for your mortgage. If you add something extra to your mortgage payment, as I discussed in Chapter Eight, make that automatic too!

6. Pay all your monthly bills automatically.

There are two kinds of monthly bills: regular ones that are always the same amount (like mortgage, rent, or car payments) and those where the balance due varies (like phone bills, electric bills, or cable and Internet charges). In many cases, you can automate payment of the bills that are a fixed cost by using your bank's pre-authorized bill-paying service to have them automatically debited from your chequing account each month. (You may have to set up a premium account and pay a monthly fee that covers this and other services.) And you can automate payment of the variable ones by arranging to have them charged to one of your credit cards. As long as you keep your chequing account adequately funded and you have sufficient credit available on your card you won't ever miss a payment due date. My entire financial life is automated this way. As a result, all my bills are always paid on time, whether I am in town or not, and I never get hit with late fees or penalties.

You've now made your financial life automatic. Congratulations! You've taken a major step forward towards becoming Debt Free for Life!

DEBT FREE FOR LIFE ACTION STEPS

❏ Set up an automatic payroll deduction to fund your retirement account as well as other savings plans.
❏ Arrange for direct deposit of your paycheque.
❏ Use your bank's online bill-paying service to automatically take care of your monthly minimum credit card payments and other regular bills.

CHAPTER FIFTEEN

FIND THE MONEY! 7 SIMPLE WAYS TO FIND HUNDREDS OF DOLLARS (MAYBE THOUSANDS) IN LESS THAN AN HOUR

Canadians leave millions of dollars lying around in unclaimed accounts that they've either forgotten about or never knew they had. From unclaimed bank accounts, the Bank of Canada is holding about $395 million. There's also another $25 million available in unclaimed tax refunds.

Now that you are motivated to get out of debt for good, I know you'll want to look for extra money to add to your debt payments. With this in mind, I decided to write this chapter and share with you some tools that may help you "find the money"—money that you may already have but don't know about.

I assume that sentence above about the $395 million in unclaimed bank balances got your attention. Well, it's true. Millions of dollars in unclaimed assets are sitting in the coffers of the Bank of Canada, Canada Revenue Agency, and other government cubbyholes, as well—and maybe some of it is yours. So let's take a look. Who knows—you may find some money that's just sitting out there somewhere, waiting for you.

HOW I FIRST LEARNED ABOUT
"FINDING THE MONEY"

I first learned about "finding the money" from the State Treasurer of Illinois, Judy Baar Topinka. She said her government was holding over a billion dollars in unclaimed assets from old bank accounts, retirement plans, insurance payouts, rebates, divorce settlements, tax refunds—you name it.

In Canada, a similar pile of money is sitting unclaimed from credit union accounts, bankruptcy payouts, and life insurance settlements as well as more common sources like bank accounts.

$395 MILLION IN "ABANDONED" ASSETS
ARE OUT THERE WAITING TO BE CLAIMED

According to the Bank of Canada, there is about $395 million in unclaimed balances sitting in the bank's coffers, from more than 1.1 million bank accounts. The money comes not only from bank accounts but from GICs, bank drafts, credit card balances, and term deposits. The vast majority of these accounts—more than 90% of them—hold less than $1,000. But the largest unclaimed amount is $423,598.59. There are another 153 accounts holding $25,000 or more.

I call this FOUND MONEY. Imagine how much debt we could all pay off with it? So it's worth checking to see if one of these unclaimed accounts is yours. After all, how great would it be to have an extra thousand dollars to put towards your Debt Free for Life Plan?

So please read this chapter and visit the sites I am about to share with you.

Okay enough said—let's go searching—and FIND YOUR MONEY.

Here's how.

> ## 1. Check for unredeemed bonds at the
> ## Canada Savings Bond office.

According to the Department of Finance, more than $112 million worth of old Canada Savings Bonds have never been redeemed. Canada Savings Bond staff go to great lengths to locate the owners of bonds as they mature. But for one reason or another, about 63,000 bondholders didn't get the message.

Considering that seven million Canadians own CSBs or Canada Premium Bonds, that isn't a huge number of people. But if you're one of them, you should investigate and get the money.

How do you do this? Well, let's go and find out.

Unlike forgotten bank accounts, there's no website that lists unclaimed money from mature Canada Savings Bonds. But all it takes is a phone call to find out if you have some money coming to you from uncashed bonds.

Depending on the age of the CSB, you can phone one of two numbers:

For CSBs from series 1 to 31, you should call the Bank of Canada at 1-800-665-8650.

For CSBs from series 32 and later, you should contact the CSB office at 1-800-575-5151.

You'll have to verify your identity and provide either the serial numbers of the bonds or the date when you bought them.

Again, it's all FREE and it can lead to FREE MONEY!

2. Check with the Bank of Canada's
unclaimed balances service.

As much fun as it is to find money from uncashed Canada
Savings Bonds, it's equally fun to find money the banks may
be holding for you. Remember that savings account you
opened up with your parents as a kid? Did you ever cash it
out? What about the bank account you first opened up when
you got married, or that savings account your grandmother
opened for your kids to pay for their university tuition?

The fact is that people move, change jobs, get married,
change their names, get divorced, change their names again,
move to another country, die—you name it. Every single day,
money gets lost at the banks.

And it's not simply because people forget. These days, if
there is no activity on a bank account, Canadian banks must
notify the account holder in writing after two years and again
after five years. After nine years, the Office of the Superintendent
of Financial Institutions publishes the names of the owners of
all unclaimed balances worth $10 or more in the *Canada
Gazette*, available at all public libraries. In the tenth year, the
accounts are transferred to the Bank of Canada.

Since Canadians move around a lot and seldom check the
Canada Gazette, many of these accounts remain unclaimed.
Here's how to find out if one of them is yours.

First, go to the website of the Bank of Canada (**www.bank-
banque-canada.ca**). In the drop-down menu under "Services"
in the list at the top of the page, click on "Unclaimed Balances."
You'll find a search form there that you can use to see quickly
if your name is on any of the unclaimed accounts.

The whole process takes about a minute. And it's absolutely
FREE.

One final note: If you deposited your forgotten money at a credit union rather than a bank, you won't find it by checking with the Bank of Canada. It deals only with federally regulated financial institutions. Credit unions are provincially regulated.

To track down an account at a credit union, you should start with the branch and then the head office of the credit union. In Nova Scotia, you can also check an online database of unclaimed accounts at:

www.nscudic.org/unclaimedbalances/index.html

The only other provinces that administer centralized online databases of unclaimed property are B.C. (**www. unclaimedpropertybc.ca/**) and Quebec (**www.revenu.gouv. qc.ca/en/sepf/services/sgp_bnr/default.aspx**).

---

3. Check for unclaimed refunds with Canada Revenue Agency.

Am I really suggesting that you check with the CRA to see if they have any money for you?

Yes, that's exactly what I'm suggesting—and, yes, I mean it.

At last report, the CRA had a stack of refund cheques that it couldn't deliver or that no one claimed. There were almost 40,000 cheques in the stack, and they were worth more than $25 million. Maybe one of them is yours.

First, I want you to contact your local Canada Revenue Agency office. You can find them listed at *www.cra-arc.gc.ca/ cntct/tso-bsf-eng.html*.

The CRA not only keeps uncashed cheques for tax refunds, but also has other stacks of cheques for GST credits and Canada Child Tax benefits.

Because of privacy laws, the CRA can't post this information on a website. That's why you have to contact a CRA office directly, by phone, and ask for instructions on making a claim.

4. Check for unclaimed bankruptcy dividends.

I've already told you how you can file for bankruptcy. Now I'm going to tell you how you can collect when someone else goes bankrupt and you might have missed the news.

If you're a creditor of someone who either declares bankruptcy or files a proposal, which we discussed in Chapter Thirteen, you might not have given your contact information to the trustee or administrator. With no way to find you, the trustee or administrator can't deliver the cheque to you when the time comes to hand out the assets of the financially strapped individual or company.

These payments are called dividends, and even though they usually amount to a fraction of the total debt owed to creditors, they are still worth something. So it's worth your while to find out if you have some money coming to you.

A lot of people, it seems, haven't done this. According to the Office of the Superintendent of Bankruptcy, there are almost 80,000 unclaimed dividends in the OSB's database, worth $14.6 million. The largest single unclaimed amount is $179,636.

If you think one of these unclaimed dividends is yours, go to the OSB website and type your name or the debtor's name into the unclaimed funds database. The database is located at: **www.ic.gc.ca/cgi-bin/sc_mrksv/bnkrptcy/ud/ud_srch.pl.**

If you think you've found an unclaimed dividend, you'll have to pay $30 to get it, even if your request is not approved. You do this by filing a Proof of Claim with the trustee.

You'll find detailed instructions on searching for an unclaimed dividend and filing a Proof of Claim at the OSB website.

> ### 5. Check with the Canadian Life & Health Insurance Association.

Chances are, if you've forgotten about bank balances, tax refunds. or unredeemed savings bonds, you've got something better to think about. However, you'll have to think promptly about finding unclaimed insurance payouts. That's because there's a limit on the amount of time that can pass before you're out of luck.

If a person dies and you think you're entitled to a payment from a life insurance policy that you can't find, you have to apply for a search within two years of the death. And before you do this, the Ombudsman for Life & Health Insurance suggests that you do your homework.

Make sure that you've looked everywhere for the policy: safety deposit boxes, desk drawers, under the bed, etc. Check the deceased person's bank accounts for withdrawals that look as if they might apply to a life insurance policy. Contact the person's insurance agent and the human resources office of the person's employer. You'll find more tips at the Ombudsman's website: **www.olhi.ca/policy_search.html**.

If you still think that you have money coming to you under the deceased person's insurance policy, you can file a request for a policy search. It's available at the Ombudsman's website, as well. The Ombudsman's office will then contact member companies, which receive 99% of the life insurance premiums in Canada, and ask them to search for the missing policy.

Although it seems onerous, it's worth doing this search if you think you have some money coming to you. About one in five people succeeds in tracking down a payment, for amounts ranging from $3,500 to more than $200,000.

---

6. Check with your province's unclaimed property office.

As I mentioned earlier, if you live in Quebec or British Columbia, you can check the website where your province records unclaimed property of all kinds, from unpaid proceeds from court decisions to unpaid wages.

In B.C., the Unclaimed Property Society administers a website at:

www.unclaimedpropertybc.ca.

In Quebec, the Register of Unclaimed Property lists a range of property from inactive bank accounts and unclaimed inheritances to vehicles abandoned on public highways. You can check for property that you might be entitled to at:

www.revenu.gouv.qc.ca/en/sepf/services/sgp_bnr/ default.aspx

Ontario doesn't operate an unclaimed property office, but you can check to see if you're entitled to an inheritance from someone who died without a will, by checking with the Office of the Public Guardian and Trustee (OPGT):

www.attorneygeneral.jus.gov.on.ca/english/family/pgt/ heirclaim.asp

You may choose to do this using an agent. If you do, you should know that the law in Ontario places a limit on the fee that an agent can charge of 10% of the compensation eventually collected.

To succeed in claiming an inheritance, you have to prove who you are with sworn affidavits from two people. If you're not sure if a relative left you an inheritance, you have to check first with the Ontario Court nearest to your relative's home.

You'll find more detailed advice on finding an inheritance at the OPGT website.

7. Check for unused gift cards and gift certificates.

How many times have you received a gift card and never bothered to use it or used only part of it—or just flat out lost it? I know I do that all the time. And so do a lot of people. Hard to believe—but true, so go and take a look and find some of your money today!

DEBT FREE FOR LIFE SUCCESS STORY

David, I read many of your books. *Start Late, Finish Rich* gave me my first financial epiphany and got me to take charge of my financial life. Since reading it, I have paid off over $60,000 in debt and I expect have my last credit card paid off by next June. Go Green Finish Rich helped me to decrease my utilities bills by 25%. And an unexpected surprise occurred when I read *Start Over, Finish Rich*—which I did in one sitting. When I was reading about government offices holding unclaimed assets, I immediately put the book down, picked up my laptop and quickly checked the different jurisdictions I had lived in. Imagine my surprise when I found $76.43 held for me!

> I feel incredibly happy and excited about my future now that I have a firm grasp on my finances. Thank you so much!
>
> **Jane J.**
> **Fort Bragg, CA**

PLEASE TELL ME IF YOU FOUND SOME MONEY!

Okay, now that you've learned the secrets to finding lost or forgotten money that may be yours, you have no excuse not to go out and start looking.

Honestly, the best part of my day is reading the success stories that readers send me. If you wind up finding some money you never knew you had, please head over to **www.facebook.com/davidbach** and post what happened or send us a video clip You can also e-mail me at **success@finishrich.com** and let me know what happened. Your success story may inspire someone else to try this!

DEBT FREE FOR LIFE ACTION STEPS

❑ Check with the Canada Savings Bond office to see if you own any unredeemed Savings Bonds you've forgotten about.

❑ Visit **www.bank-banque-canada.ca** to see if you have money in an unclaimed bank account.

❑ Visit **www.ic.gc.ca/cgi-bin/sc_mrksv/bnkrptcy/ud/ud_srch.pl** to see if you have any money coming to you from a bankrupt individual or company.

❑ And don't forget to check with the CRA to see it might be holding an unclaimed refund for you.

A FINAL WORD

FROM IN DEBT TO DEBT FREE—
AND A DREAM TRIP—ALL IN LESS THAN A YEAR

As I was finishing up this book, I received an email from a reader named Farren. Farren was in the middle of taking my FinishRich Coaching Program, and he was writing to let me know that even though he hadn't yet finished the course, his entire life had already completely changed. In less than eight months, he had gone from being stressed out over his finances to being out of credit card debt and on his way to a dream trip—seven weeks in Australia with his wife and two young sons.

As I read his email, it really hit me—it's all about mindset and action. Farren's mindset had changed, and as a result so had his actions.

Here's the original e-mail Farren sent me. I want you to read it because there's so much in it to learn from. You too can enjoy this type of success.

David, I just wanted to send a quick email to thank you once again for providing a great product/service and resource. I have listened to the CDs, watched the DVDs, read your book "Start Over Finish Rich," implemented the strategies, and changed my mindset!

In less than a year, we've paid off $12,000 in American Express credit card debt, drastically reduced our monthly expenses, created a financial future with less stress, and—

*drum roll, please—the most exciting thing is that we are taking
7 weeks off for a family trip to Australia! (And I was able to
pay cash for the $6k airfare!) My wife and two boys age 5 and 8
years old are so excited.*

*I took a picture of our little home savings jar that we used
as a visual reminder for our kids and ourselves to see what we
were saving for and how much we were saving. My kids are
now excited to save. When they find a nickel or a penny—even
change in my car—they run to the kitchen to put money into
our "Australia Fund!"*

*Really life-changing stuff ... so thanks to you and your team
for their financial wisdom. These are troubled times for some,
but with a plan and a coach, there's nothing stopping you from
the greatest life change you can do ... understanding how to be
financially free!*

Cheers to you guys and "hi 5"! Thanks again!

Live your dream,

Farren West

I wrote back to Farren immediately, telling him how
amazing I thought his email was. It was as if he had just read
Debt Free for Life. "I love how you changed your mindset, took
action, and involved your family!" I wrote him. "You are an
amazing example of how quickly you can get out of debt and
start LIVING YOUR DREAMS. Nearly two months in
Australia—sounds incredible!"

Farren's response was as inspiring as his first note:

*We have just barely implemented your systems and still have
made significant changes and progress. But it's really like you
said—it's all about mindset and action. If you are married,
you really have to have a "come to Jesus" meeting with your*

significant other. Look at ways you are both wasting money, create a goal, and go after it. A visual reminder like the jar in our kitchen also really helps. And if you can get the kids involved and excited, that can make all of the difference.

YOU COULD BE THE NEXT GREAT SUCCESS STORY!

Farren's story touches me for many reasons—and maybe it touches you, too.

First, even though Farren was in debt, he was still willing to invest in himself to learn more about handling money and building wealth. With the benefit of what he learned, he changed his mindset and he took action. He'd didn't over-think it—he just got going. He also involved his whole family in his dream of being debt free. He sat down with his wife and had the hard talk about looking for ways to cut back on spending. Then they created a visual aid (the money jar) to help them save money—and they got their kids to participate. As a result of all this, in just eight months, Farren was able to pay off a $12,000 credit card debt—and on top of that save enough to be able to pay cash for $6,000 in plane tickets and take his family on a two-month dream trip to Australia.

I mean, really—it's a story that can make you jealous. Here's a couple in debt, struggling to keep their heads above water, and in less than a year their whole life is turned around—simply as a result of changing their mindset and taking action (plus a little bit of coaching and education).

There is another thing about Farren's story that really touched me. When I received his email, I was staying at a very nice hotel in Del Mar, California, where I wrote a lot of this book. That particular day I happened to be having lunch with a close friend who is very well off. My friend was telling me how he hoped he could make enough money over the next four years to be able to take six months off. Now, my friend is worth at least a few million dollars, so I said to him, "Steve, you could take that time off now. Look at this email I just got. This guy was up to his eyeballs in credit card debt six months ago, and now he's paid it off and figured out how to take seven weeks off. If this guy can pull this off in less than a year, there's no reason you need to wait four years to go for your dream."

My friend read Farren's email—and it immediately got him thinking. He looked up at me and said, "You're so right. It really *is* all about mindset. Maybe I *can* do this sooner than in four years." He shook his head and laughed. "When your book is done, send it to me," he added. "I need to read it."

IF FARREN CAN DO IT, WHY CAN'T YOU?

So now back to you! I really hope this book has given you the tools and the mindset you need to take action to live DEBT FREE FOR LIFE. Stories from readers like Farren are why I keep doing what I do—and I hope that if you achieve success, you too will share your story with me. You can email me at **success@finishrich.com** or through our website at **www.finishrich.com** or **www.facebook.com/davidbach**. Who knows, I might surprise you and write back to you right away.

Real success stories from real people are incredibly compelling. When you read stories like Farren's, part of you has to think, "Why not me? If they can do this, why can't I?" That's simply how our brains work. Most of us have a competitive instinct that says, "If he can do that, so can I." That's your gut speaking to you. And trust me when I tell you that your gut is right!

There are literally thousands of success stories on our website. Take a few minutes to read through some of them. I'll bet they leave you feeling even more motivated to take action than you already are.

SO NOW GET GOING

"The way to get started is to quit talking and begin doing."
—**Walt Disney**

I really can't think of a better quote with which to end this book—and for you to begin your journey towards being Debt Free for Life—than these words by Walt Disney. Ironically, as I type these final paragraphs, I'm getting ready to take my son Jack to Disneyland for his seventh birthday tomorrow. Disney was a dreamer. He was turned down by hundreds of banks, and it took him years to make his dream come true. But he was also more than a dreamer. He was a "doer" too. And thanks to his doing, his dream became a reality—one that the world has been enjoying for generations.

Now consider your dream. What is it? It doesn't need to be as big as building Disneyland. Your dream may simply be to be able to pay off your credit card debts over the next few years. Well, understand this—it can be done. You now have the tools to do it and to calculate your "Debt Freedom Day."

What about your mortgage? Did my tips on how to pay off your mortgage early inspire you to change how you make your payments (either by starting a biweekly plan or adding an extra month's payment at the end of each year)? Well, then, get going!

Student loans got you down? Did you use the information I gave you to make better decisions on paying it down faster? How about the interest on those credit cards you have? Did you use the tools in the book to lower your rate as I suggested? Did you pick up the phone and try to negotiate a better deal? Did you give up after one call or did you keep trying?

Maybe you liked the idea of getting a trained counsellor to guide you out of debt—and maybe help you set up a Debt Management Plan?. If so, did you do something about it—or are you still waiting? *Don't wait any longer.*

Maybe you were surprised by how easy it is to make your financial life AUTOMATIC. Did you read my plan and think, "This is really simple! I could do this!" So *did* you do it? If not, get doing.

And how about all those great websites I listed where you can go to "find your money." Have you checked out any of them out to see if your money is sitting in a government account somewhere? What have you got to lose? Every day I get emails from people who have found money using these free sites. *Go try them.* You've got a much better chance of finding some lost money that belongs to you than you have of winning the lottery. So spend an hour searching.

In the end, whichever part of the DEBT FREE FOR LIFE program got you excited, there is one question I want you to ask yourself right now.

Why not?

WHY NOT YOU—RIGHT NOW—START TODAY!

Why not you? Right now! Why not be one of the many people who will read this book and DECIDE today to begin DOING.

You are ready to act. You now have so much knowledge about debt that you could actually start helping others. But first, help yourself! If you try one of my suggestions and you don't like the results, you can always go back to what you were doing before.

The truth is I don't think you will ever go back. Very few people who truly DECIDE to be debt free change their minds later on and decide that they liked being in debt better. I started this book talking about our grandparents and great-grandparents who survived and ultimately thrived following the Great Depression. Think back on them now. I know my grandparents didn't change their mind about freeing themselves from debt. My grandmother Rose decided to be debt free—and she died debt free, a millionaire. She passed her knowledge of being debt free and investing to her family, and she shaped not only her destiny but also that of her children, grandchildren, and great-grandchildren.

Why not you? Why not start today? **You could change your destiny today.** I truly believe you will be happier with less debt—and I know that in just three to five years, if you follow the systems I have laid out in this book, your entire financial life will be better. You'll have less stress—and you'll probably be healthier too. One interesting thing I've noticed is that many of my readers who lose debt also lose weight. Remember Nicole's success story back in Chapter One? Whenever she thinks about spending money on a snack, she now asks herself, "Is this purchase really necessary?" As a result, she has saved more than $6,000 in six months—and lost 21 pounds! Cool story—right? Why not you?

BET ON YOURSELF TO WIN—
AND ENJOY THE JOURNEY

In truth, the DEBT FREE FOR LIFE process isn't just about the result—it's also about the journey. As soon as you start working on paying down your debt, you will begin to feel better. As you see yourself making progress, each day will seem a little freer, a little less stressful, a little more joyful.

I know you bought this book and took the time to read it because you are special—because you believe in yourself. People who are cynical or pessimistic generally don't buy books about having a better life. They simply say, "That won't work for me" and move on.

That's not you. You believe in yourself. And you should. Tom Hanks, the Oscar-winning actor, once said something that changed my life forever. He was asked what he regarded as the best part of his success. Now, Tom Hanks has won so many awards, starred in so many successful movies, had such an amazing career. But out of all that, what do you think he identified as his greatest accomplishment? He said it was that although a lot of people didn't believe he could do it, he *did* believe. And not only did he believe, but he decided to bet on himself to win. And guess what? It worked!

Just typing that gives me shivers. Around the time I heard Hanks say that, I had a dream of my own. It was to write a book called *Smart Women Finish Rich*. Just about everyone told me it was a dumb idea—and I shouldn't do it. You now hold my twelfth book in your hand (a book, by the way, that took me five years to convince my publisher to let me do). At the end of the day, I "bet on myself to win"—and that has made all the difference in my life.

Like Tom Hanks, I say, "Bet on yourself to win!" If that's the only thing you get from this book, then reading it was worth it. There really is no greater gift than this realization. And you deserve it.

So good luck on your journey. And please email me at **success@finishrich.com** if this book touches you or changes your life for the better. Also, please join our community at **www.finishrich.com** or **www.facebook.com/davidbach** so we can keep in touch. Almost every day on my website I post new information that can help you live and finish rich.

Until we meet again, enjoy the sweetness of your life and, truly, enjoy the journey!

Make this life of yours special—because it is.

Your friend,
David Bach

INDEX

ABOUT THE AUTHOR

David Bach has helped millions of people around the world take action to live and finish rich. He is one of the most popular and prolific financial authors of our time, with ten consecutive national bestsellers, including two consecutive #1 *New York Times* bestsellers, *Start Late, Finish Rich* and *The Automatic Millionaire,* as well as the national and international bestsellers *Start Over, Finish Rich; Fight for Your Money; Go Green, Live Rich; The Automatic Millionaire Homeowner; Smart Women Finish Rich; Smart Couples Finish Rich; The Finish Rich Workbook;* and *The Automatic Millionaire Workbook.* Bach carries the unique distinction of having had four of his books appear simultaneously on the *Wall Street Journal, BusinessWeek,* and *USA Today* bestseller lists. In addition, four of Bach's books were named to *USA Today's* Best Sellers of the Year list for 2004. In all, his FinishRich Books have been published in more than 15 languages, with more than 7 million copies in print worldwide.

Bach's breakout book, *The Automatic Millionaire,* was the #1 business book of 2004, according to *BusinessWeek.* It spent thirty-one weeks on the *New York Times* bestseller list and was simultaneously number one on the bestseller lists of the *New York Times, BusinessWeek, USA Today,* and the *Wall Street Journal.* With more than a million copies in print, this simple and powerful book has been translated into 12 languages and has inspired thousands around the world to save money automatically.

Bach is regularly featured in the media. He is a regular contributor to NBC's *Today* and appears on its popular weekly "Money 911" segments. He has appeared six times on *The Oprah Winfrey Show* to share his strategies for living and finishing and has made regular appearances on NBC's *Today* and *Weekend Today* shows, CNN's *Larry King Live*, ABC's *Live with Regis and Kelly, The View*, CBS's *Early Show*, ABC News, Fox News, and CNBC. He has been profiled in many major publications, including the *New York Times, BusinessWeek, USA Today, People, Reader's Digest, Time, Financial Times*, the *Washington Post*, the *Wall Street Journal*, the *Los Angeles Times*, the *San Francisco Chronicle, Working Woman, Glamour, Family Circle*, and *Redbook*. He has been a contributor to *Redbook* magazine, *Smart Money* magazine, Yahoo! Finance, AOL Money, and Oprah.com.

David Bach is the creator of the FinishRich® Seminar series, which highlights his quick and easy-to-follow financial strategies. In just the last few years, more than half a million people have learned how to take financial action to live a life in line with their values by attending his Smart Women Finish Rich®, Smart Couples Finish Rich®, and Find the Money Seminars, which have been taught in more than 2,000 cities throughout North America by thousands of financial advisors.

An internationally renowned motivational and financial speaker, Bach regularly presents seminars for and delivers keynote addresses to the world's leading financial service firms, Fortune 500 companies, universities, and national conferences. He is the founder and chairman of FinishRich Media, a company dedicated to revolutionizing the way people learn about money. Prior to founding FinishRich Media, he was a senior vice president of Morgan Stanley and a partner of The Bach Group, which during his tenure (1993 to 2001) managed more than half a billion dollars for individual investors.

As part of his mission, David Bach is involved with many worthwhile causes, including serving on the board of Habitat for Humanity New York.

David Bach lives in New York with his family. Please visit his website at www.finishrich.com.